Babylon's Cap

Babylon's Cap

Reflections on the Book of Revelation

MICHAEL J. H. GODFREY

WITH A FOREWORD BY BRUCE W. WILSON

WIPF & STOCK · Eugene, Oregon

BABYLON'S CAP
Reflections on the Book of Revelation

Copyright © 2013 Michael J. H. Godfrey. All rights reserved. Except for brief quotations in critical publications or reviews, no part of this book may be reproduced in any manner without prior written permission from the publisher. Write: Permissions, Wipf and Stock Publishers, 199 W. 8th Ave., Suite 3, Eugene, OR 97401.

Wipf & Stock
An Imprint of Wipf and Stock Publishers
199 W. 8th Ave., Suite 3
Eugene, OR 97401
www.wipfandstock.com

ISBN 13: 978-1-62032-967-2

Manufactured in the U.S.A.

Unless otherwise noted, Bible quotations are taken from the New Revised Standard Version Bible, © 1989, Division of Christian Education of the National Council of the Churches of Christ in the United States of America. Used by permission. All rights reserved.

Material from the following publications has been used with permission:
Revelation (Sacra Pagina 16) by Wilfrid J. Harrington (Liturgical Press, 1993).
True Spirit by Jessica Watson (Hachette, 2010).
Collected Poems 1909-1962, by T. S. Eliot (Faber and Faber, 1963).

Ki a Ani
Ko tōna utu hoki kei runga noa atu i tō ngā rupi
(Ngā Whakataukī 31.10b)

Contents

Foreword ix
Preface xiii

1. An Introduction to Apocalyptic 1

2. Write This Down! The Letters to the Churches (Rev 1:1—3:22) 16

3. Riders of the Apocalypse and Other Lurid Scenes (Rev 4:1—9:21) 44

4. Shock and Awe (Rev 10:1—14:20) 65

5. It Is Done! (Rev 15:1—20:15) 104

6. God's Yes (Rev 21:1—End) 126

Bibliography 141

Foreword

ARMAGEDDON AND APOCALYPSE ARE words much in current use to describe frightening forces of ultimate destruction, especially the frightening possibilities of fast-burn annihilation through nuclear warfare and slow-burn annihilation through human-produced global warming.

Such use of both words, surprisingly I suspect for modern writers and readers, derives from the last book of the Bible—the Revelation to John. The book, also known as The Apocalypse of John, recounts John's visionary experiences of the divine. Apocalypse itself literally means "revelation" but is also the name of the Book of Revelation's Hebrew-Christian literary style characterized by fantastical imagery. Armageddon is the site, in the book of Revelation, of a destructive war enveloping all the nations of the earth summoned to battle by demonic spirits. As the first age in history possessing the means to destroy the world and ourselves, it is little wonder that we draw upon words of epic biblical proportion to express such enormity.

Yet even amongst Christians, with the exceptions of conservative evangelicals and fundamentalists, few read and know the Book of Revelation today. Our secular language may draw upon its spectacular imagery to express its deepest forebodings, but secularists know its teachings, if at all, only via radically conservative Christians, especially in the US, who use it to interpret events associated with Israel and the Middle East that supposedly foretell Divine judgment and the end of the world. Invariably this Divine judgment falls on the heads of supposedly wicked others, not on the evangelical or fundamentalist interpreters themselves. So then, what does the Book of Revelation have to say to us today: anything? This book is about that question.

Rightly, Michael Godfrey explains to his readers that writings in the apocalyptic style are part of what the Bible calls prophecy, and that the core purpose of prophecy is not predicting the future but interpreting the present in the light of God's promised future. That future, according to the revelation to John, is the final end of all injustice, evil, wickedness, suffering,

Foreword

and death in the triumph of God through Jesus (the slain lamb) ushering in a new age of love, justice, tender care, peace, and ever-flowing life.

When we use the word "apocalyptic" in the modern sense of foreboding destructiveness and of fearful evils and wickedness, then every age of history is haunted by Armageddons and apocalypses, whether it be earthquake, tsunami, flood, famine, plague, flu pandemic, mayhem, murder, spear, sword, Kalashnikov, tank, missile, or hydrogen bomb. And for all of us in every age, our human bodily life ends in death.

With its fantastical, bizarre, apocalyptic imagery, stretching but also exposing the limits of human imagination, the book of Revelation portrays visions of hope for a just, peaceful, joyous, life-filled world that is yet to come. But is it all delusion, pie-in-the-sky-when-you-die wishful sentimentality?

Whether it be St. John's apocalyptic vision or St. Paul's somewhat more prosaic picture where humanity and the creation itself groan with desire for transformation into God's new world, one clear element of the Christian hope is an unabashed, unashamed rejection of this present world, in spite of many redeeming qualities, as ultimately unjust, violent, cruel, death-ridden, and without hope. Current shallow secular and atheistic optimism—from carnal obsession and consumerism to nature aestheticism and salvation through science—is a repressive denial of this bleak vision. This dark side of Christian hope includes the destruction of evil and wickedness vividly portrayed by John's vision of seven angels pouring seven golden bowls of the wrath of God upon the earth.

This book masterfully places the Christian hope of John's Revelation in the midst of the philosophical, political, social, artistic, and general culture of today's secular West. In this sense, Michael Godfrey has written a very "with it" book. He insists that the wrath of God is about the destruction of wickedness, not of the wicked; the latter is used as a ploy by the self-righteous of every age, from homophobes to terrorists and warmongers, claiming God is on their side empowering and justifying hatred, judgment, and destruction of their enemies.

Those who thus abuse the negative side of Christian hope, as Godfrey makes clear, need reminding that the original recipients of John's Apocalypse were suffering victims, not powerful victimizers. Revelation is best read, he says, not only out aloud, the way its first recipients would have known it, but by imagining that one is a suffering victim of persecution by an all-powerful oppressor. To read it from the point of view of a person of power, using it to condemn and judge others, fatally reverses its intended meaning.

Foreword

John's vision encouraged persecuted ancient Christians to persevere in trusting God's promise of a new age, even though their spiritual commitment provided—as all Christians in every age have subsequently learnt—no exemption from the common sorrows, sufferings, and injustices of their time. He does not invite his hearers to escape into a heavenly dream world but to live in this present world with endurance and hope, so that God's promise about future transformation of the world, a new heaven and a new earth, becomes also a transforming vision for the here and now. As it is said, human beings can endure just about anything so long as there is hope.

Whether the *end* of history, or the *end* of the world, or the *end* of you and me in the death of our bodies, the meaning or the unmeaning of *the end*, one's eschatology, is not a question of "faith," at least not in the sense of choosing to believe one thing or choosing to believe another thing, as if mere belief creates or destroys what is real. That literally would be madness, where all things are the same, equally real or unreal.

To a modern secularist or atheist, John's vision, with its exotic apocalyptic literary style, may itself seem thoroughly mad, a grand psychedelic or psychotic hallucination divorced from reality. But the heart of his vision, beginning with the seven letters to seven actual first-century churches, is about trust not belief, about yes and about no. Trust and belief are related but are not the same. It is theologically and spiritually more accurate to say that the Christian religion calls upon humanity to *trust* in the God of Jesus than to believe in the God of Jesus.

Is the end of this world, how and whenever it may come, and our own individual end, a yes or a no? Unlike the unreflective, consumer, diversionary therapy of the modern secular West saying neither yes nor no, John's vision says Yes and Yes. Yes to God's promised new age and Yes to the final destruction of this age of injustice, wickedness, evil, suffering, and death. John's vision calls upon all his hearers and readers to say Yes to the Divine Yes, a question of trust but also of belief.

The God whom John calls upon his readers to trust is not any god, and not the god of modern philosophical debate, but God as revealed in the story of Jesus of Nazareth, his teachings, sufferings, death, and resurrection. It is certainly not god as an impersonal, solely matter-energy Being on its way to final entropy where everything is statically the same and the personal is annihilated. That is a very different god with a very different eschatology for which trust has little meaning at all. In the culture of the West, this god and its eschatology is beginning to replace the God of biblical

Foreword

hope, and one must at the very least wonder if this is not the real cause of the West's epidemic of psychic depression. An Indigenous Australian might well ask—is the white man losing his dreaming?

Michael Godfrey has written a bold book, a book that will challenge many assumptions of a Christian as well as a secular-relativist reader, a book that is as much about social justice as prayer or meditation. But above all it is a bold book because it unfashionably centers upon heaven not earth, on a world to come, not the here and now. It is a book that situates the Apocalypse of St. John firmly in a cultural and intellectual world familiar to anyone at home in our digital age. A book also that aptly encapsulates Jesus' prayer "Thy will be done in earth as it is in heaven." Godfrey says that at the heart of his own life and being is John's vision of the new heaven and the new earth transcending the first heaven and the first earth as the latter pass away. His book is not only bold but also timely, beginning to address a great modern neglect.

B. W. Wilson
Anglican Bishop of Bathurst, 1989–2000

Preface

THIS SMALL BOOK GREW out of a chain of circumstances. Perhaps it began, as I mention later, when my erstwhile rowing coach, Dr. Chris Harper, wrote to me early in 1979, quoting John's recollection of Jesus' words of invitation, "Listen! I am standing at the door, knocking; if you hear my voice and open the door, I will come in to you and eat with you, and you with me" (Rev 3.20). It was in no small part through Chris's reference to those words that I surrendered my adolescent atheism and turned to Christ. For that I will be ever grateful—it was a privilege to share my fiftieth birthday with Chris and his wife Judy, together with my wife Anne and our sons, thirty years after he cited these words to me.

In more direct terms, this book began during a five-year stint as the vicar of a provincial city parish in the North Island of New Zealand. The people of Christ Church, Whangarei patiently humored me while I attempted to hammer them with my own form of what I hope was bibliocentric preaching. A significant group of those hardy fellow-travelers joined me week by week for analyses and criticisms of the ideas I had floated in my sermons. During Lent and Advent I decided to push them further, through studies of the shape of the liturgy, the creed, Paul's letters, and the book we call Hebrews. Before I knew I was returning to Australia, I threatened them with a study on the Book of Revelation, but these reflections were in the end written during my first year in a new parish, a new faith community in the rural mango belt south of Darwin. I inflicted them on new fellow-travelers, but that is often the way of ministry. I hope I have not bewildered the people of Fred's Pass too much!

This is not intended as a scholarly work. I hope I have engaged sufficiently with far greater scholars than I could ever be in order to generate my own thoughts: theirs, not mine, is the scholarship; mine, not theirs, are the subsequent musings! My varying degrees of debt to David Aune, Richard Bauckham, Eugene Boring, Wilfrid Harrington, Robert Mounce, Christopher Rowland, and others will be evident to anyone who knows the field of Revelation research; I can only thank them for the herculean efforts they each have made. John the Seer's Apocalypse is a minefield, and they have made navigation through it at least possible to a twenty-first-century biblical reader.

There are other, more indirect influences here, too. Jürgen Moltmann, though he never knew me (he passed me the salt, once, when I asked him to at Melbourne's Trinity College), taught me how to read both Bible and history. My entire pastoral ministry since I was ordained twenty-five years ago has had Moltmann's theology of the cross pulsing through its veins. Or at least I hope it has, because I believe it is that which has led me between my Scylla and Charybdis. I will be ever grateful for the first time I picked up *The Crucified God*. That book changed my life at least as much as Chris Harper's citation of the Book of Revelation five years earlier, and many days and weeks have been spent in subsequent years reading his writings.

It was the erstwhile Director of Trinity Theological College in Melbourne, R. W. A. (Dick) McKinney, who introduced me both figuratively and, as it happened, literally, to Moltmann. Dick was a controversial man, but to me he will always be the figure who arrived with *le mot juste* (or "word on target"), as I floundered in theological formation. He died far too young: oh to have chewed the fat and sipped good wine with Dick and his wife Margie, also gone far too young, as I was formulating the ideas that became this book. He was an inspirational figure in my life, for which I will be ever grateful. Above all, although he was a systematician, he taught me the centrality of the text, that the Bible is not merely, as one of my colleagues put it, "an old book," but for all its flaws it is the yardstick of effective *praxis* (theologians like this word to describe "theologically informed" Christian practice) in the world in which I have been called to live. I hope these reflections—for that is what they are—on the Apocalypse of John are a tribute to the focus Dick gave me as I tried to find my way into meaningful pastoral ministry in a post-modern world.

My thanks go to Bishop Bruce Wilson for the encouraging Foreword that he has taken time to write for me, and for being a conduit of wisdom and encouragement during some difficult times in my own life. Although I served as a priest in Bruce's diocese for only three years, they were years in which I was inspired by the potential for episcopal leadership to lift God's people from banality to energized service of the gospel. I thank him for the reminder that there are church leaders who take time to reflect meaningfully on their faith, Bible in one hand and newspapers or other media in

Preface

the other, as they seek to proclaim Christ in and to a post-modern world. Of course Bruce is not the only one (Rowan Williams comes to mind), but Bruce's leadership was inspirational, and he re-connected me to the proclamation task in which we all share. I was citing his book long before I asked him to write a Foreword.

I am these days chaplain at a large coeducational secondary school, Kormilda College, in Australia's remote Northern Territory. The students often receive—hopefully in age-adjusted format—the outcome of my lifetime of biblical reflections. I learn far more from the students than they do from me, and I want to put on record my thanks to them, and to my colleagues on staff, for keeping me more or less in touch with a changing world. In particular I pay my respects to the Indigenous students, many from remote and disadvantaged communities, together with their families and care-givers: as we will note occasionally in the pages that follow, theirs is a world carrying deep scars from a colonial past, inflicted on them by those who may well have perpetrated once again, however inadvertently, all the evil of Babylon and its cap (often in the name of Jesus). I can only admire the tenacity of these communities and their young, and pray that by the grace of God their future is filled far more with justice and compassion than has been their past two hundred or so years, since Europeans devastated their infrastructures and lifestyles.

I thank, too, the people of the faith community of the Church of the Emmanuel at Gunbalanya (Oenpelli) in Arnhem Land in Australia's Northern Territory, especially Rev. Lois Nadjamerrek and her sister Hagar Bulliwana. These people have reminded me patiently and authentically that Jesus is not a Western construct but a living, loving redeemer who continuously brings them hope in often very demanding circumstances. Out there, in the ancient terrain, they live and practice their faith in circumstances too often neglected or patronized not only by politicians but by all of us who dwell in air-conditioned comfort, where (as Klaus Klostermaier once observed drily from a similarly ancient context) "no goats die of heat stroke."[1]

Others have helped in less dramatic ways. Dr. Lisa Emerson, of Massey University, has repeatedly encouraged me in my writing, and she has provided helpful corrective commentary as I have tried to string words together. Leisa Lance has proofread this text with the same skilled critical eye she brought to an earlier wrestling match with my doctoral thesis—and together with her husband Richard Lance has provided much fruit of the

---

1. Klostermaier, *Hindu and Christian*, 48.

Preface

grape to enhance conversation and reflection. Sheila Swarbrick, warden of the aforementioned parish of Whangarei, has also cast a critical eye over the manuscript, protecting me from typological gaffes. Christopher Honoré, of St. John's College in Auckland, provided valuable feedback, having likewise read the manuscript. The members of my study group at Christ Church, Whangarei provided inspirational dialogue and engagement with Bible and tradition, leading to this project, while my new parishioners at the Church of the Good Shepherd, south of Darwin in Australia's challenging Northern Territory, humored me while I imposed my ideas on them: thank you for your patience. I wish to record, too, a large vote of thanks to my editor, Kristin Argall, who fine-tuned these pages and rescued me from many embarrassing blunders. I must emphasize though, that mistakes that remain in these pages are utterly my own.

Family is a nebulous concept in a post-modern age, and mine is no exception. As the father of six daughters from a first marriage and two sons from a second, I have some insight into the pressures faced by new generations. While I cannot claim any of the eight share my enthusiasm for biblical theology, perhaps the fact that all of them, so far, have headed off into caring professions (even if for some the main recipient of care are German Shepherds and thoroughbred racehorses) suggests that some of the values biblical authors held dear still permeate the alleged self-centered worlds of Gen-X, Y, perhaps even Z. To Vanessa, Natasha, Rosalind, Caitlin, Johanna, Phoebe, Julian, and Jonty: *arohanui, tōku tamariki*. Now there's a grandson . . . here's hoping young Zac McArdle will find, somewhere, sometime, the magnificence not only of this heaven and earth, but the one that is yet to come.

Above all I thank Rev. Anne van Gend, my wife. For years she journeyed with me through studies towards a doctorate in biblical theology. Now, as she strives towards completion of her own doctoral dissertation, she has found time still to encourage my obsession with these reflections—another way of saying that she has found time to massage this male ego, despite her mammoth tasks at home and at work. *Kia kaha, Ani.*

Darwin

1

An Introduction to Apocalyptic

READING APOCALYPTIC

You may recall the Francis Ford Coppola movie *Apocalypse Now*. Based on Joseph Conrad's novel *Heart of Darkness*, it tells the story of the search for renegade Special Forces colonel Walter Kurtz (played by Brando, no less!). The title alludes more to the brutality and fearful horror of unfolding events than to any religious, much less biblical theme, but it was symptomatic of a theme emergent in late twentieth-century literature and arts. Fundamentalist Christian writers such as the influential American evangelical Timothy LaHaye, with ghostwriter Jerry Jenkins, popularized LaHaye's particular versions of apocalyptic in his influential *Left Behind* series of novels and films. Apocalyptic expectations reached frenzied peaks as the Western calendar approached the year 2000, and they have enjoyed subsequent minor peaks as Christian doomsday prophet Harold Camping publicized his speculations and as the Mayan Calendar approached the end of its chronological cycle.

The word "apocalypse" and its derivatives were given a new energy and urgency not only as the second millennia of Christianity drew to a close, but as humanity recognized, after Hiroshima and Nagasaki, its ability to destroy itself. Biblical apocalyptic specialist D. S. Russell observed "It is with reference to violence and the use of violence that the word 'apocalyptic' is perhaps most widely (and most loosely) used at this present time."[1]

---

1. D. S. Russell, *Apocalyptic*, 20.

Even in a theological context the word has lost its meaning, so that biblical theologian Oscar Cullmann can note acerbically

> the expression has a topical significance ... which tends more and more to assume a derogatory character. In this sense, it is customary to term "apocalyptic" those descriptions of the future which serve as pure speculations merely to satisfy human curiosity, without any interest in salvation.[2]

Cullmann has also noted that "Anything that simply satisfies curiosity, apart from any interest in salvation, deserves the derogatory often wrongly extended to *all* apocalyptic."[3]

This is not the original meaning of the word at all, and apocalyptic was never meant to be the preserve of what Eugene Boring calls "media 'evangelists' and the purveyors of pop-eschatological literature."[4] The Greek word appears twenty times in the Scriptures, on one occasion referring to nakedness in the Greek version of the Hebrew Scriptures (1 Sam 20:30), but generally meaning a "revelation"[5], the uncovering of that which is hidden. Revelations are not always a source of comfort, it should be said (Rom 2:5), but they take us mere mortals to a point where we share the perspective of God, or, as Moltmann puts it, encounter the promise of God.[6] John's task is to alert his listeners (for the book of Revelation was written to be heard) to a perspective different to their own: "The effect of John's visions ... is to expand his readers' world, both spatially (into heaven) and temporally (into the eschatological future), or, to put it another way, to open their world to divine transcendence."[7] If our lives are being lived out as one small story in the so-called "global north" early in the twenty-first century, with all that entails, an apocalyptic visionary's task is to help us dream a different dream, to transport us to a different story.

Transport: it is no accident that the hymn-writer H. W. Baker, in his majestic meditation on Psalm 23, spoke of "transports of delight." It is to our ears perhaps a peculiar phrase, but it means what it says: we are taken *from* one port *to* a new port, *trans*-ported. Baker was re-rendering the psalmist's words "my cup overflows." The psalmist speaks of a life "in the

---

2. Cullmann, *Salvation*, 80.
3. Ibid. 157.
4. Boring, *Revelation*, 49.
5. For example, Luke 2:32, Gal 1:12, Rev 1:1.
6. Moltmann, *Theology of Hope*, 45.
7. Bauckham, *Theology*, 7.

valley of the shadow of death," but knows of another life in which his cup "runneth over": his perspective has shifted from one port to anther port. Or, as scholars like to say these days, from one narrative to another.

In the 1997 film *A Beautiful Life*, the central character, played by the director Roberto Benigni, creates a story line to serve as an alternative to his reality of life in a concentration camp. He does so in order to protect his young son from the Nazis. He saves the boy by creating a narrative in which the child has to hide for as long as possible in order to win the prize (a German tank) in a competition. By this ruse the boy remains undetected by the Nazis, and his life is saved when, as the Allies approach, the guards run rampant through the camp in an orgy of killing. In this story the "narrative" into which the boy enters saves his life, as he escapes from the wartime narrative conducted by the Nazis.

Apocalyptic writings operate in much the same way. They were always products of times of oppression and persecution. No single period of persecution or particular event needs to be identified as the trigger for, for example, the book of Revelation. The community may have been experiencing several waves of exposure to derision and hatred, and loss of life. Nevertheless, persecution had become a part of their daily life and witness. The earliest of the apocalyptic writings, a section of the book of Daniel (the last Old Testament book to be written), was written when the Hebrew people were being persecuted, and apocalyptic served to reassure those who heard its visionary scenes that, no matter what befell them, God was in control and the opponents of God's people would get their just rewards at the hands of that same God. The writer of the apocalyptic vision effectively becomes the father in *A Beautiful Life*, and the hearers of the apocalypse become the child, protected and redeemed from harsh human experience by receiving and being shaped by an alternative narrative.

In *A Beautiful Life*, the child's "alternative narrative" was the game, with the tank as the prize. For the readers of biblical apocalypses, the prize is less tangible; in writing to the Philippians, Paul, well-versed in the language of apocalyptic, refers to "the prize of the heavenly call of God in Christ Jesus" (Phil 3:14), while in urging the Corinthian Christians to stay on task, he reminds them "Athletes exercise self-control in all things; they do it to receive a perishable garland, but we an imperishable one" (1 Cor 9:25). The language of apocalyptic is language of a future world, so that in Daniel the faithful are simply promised "everlasting life" (Dan 12:2), and Paul in 1 Thessalonians promises "we will be with the Lord forever" (1

Thess 4:17). John of Patmos is less restrained in the vision of Revelation, and his writing moves inexorably forward to a crashing crescendo:

> Then I saw a new heaven and a new earth; for the first heaven and the first earth had passed away, and the sea was no more. And I saw the holy city, the new Jerusalem, coming down out of heaven from God, prepared as a bride adorned for her husband. And I heard a loud voice from the throne saying,
> "See, the home of God is among mortals.
> He will dwell with them;
> they will be his peoples,
> and God himself will be with them;
> he will wipe every tear from their eyes.
> Death will be no more;
> mourning and crying and pain will be no more,
> for the first things have passed away."
> And the one who was seated on the throne said, "See, I am making all things new." Also he said, "Write this, for these words are trustworthy and true." Then he said to me, "It is done! I am the Alpha and the Omega, the beginning and the end. To the thirsty I will give water as a gift from the spring of the water of life. Those who conquer will inherit these things, and I will be their God and they will be my children."[8]

This is, more than any other, the passage that dwells at the heart of my own theology and faith. This magisterial vision of John of Patmos is the German tank of *A Beautiful Life*, writ large across the pages of eternity. If it is "pie in the sky," then it is a pretty good pie, and one for which the faithful have been prepared to surrender their lives for more than twenty centuries: "The term is over: the holidays have begun," says Aslan, softly, at the end of *The Last Battle*. "The dream has ended: this is the morning."[9]

If you are biblically well-rehearsed, you will notice that I ended the crescendo passage of Revelation before its final verse. There John's vision turns to those outside the community of faith, and does so with a caustic tongue: "But as for the cowardly, the faithless, the polluted, the murderers, the fornicators, the sorcerers, the idolaters, and all liars, their place will be in the lake that burns with fire and sulfur, which is the second death."[10] If

---

8. Rev 21:1–7.

9. There are innumerable editions of the Narnia Chronicles. Reference here is to the HarperCollins edition, 1998, 192. It is, however, the penultimate paragraph in any edition!

10. Rev 21:8.

we are to read apocalyptic, we will have to acknowledge that it has a dark side; but it is dark only if read from a position of power, rather than being read from a perspective informed by the powerlessness of desperation and persecution. The darkness is directed (if darkness can be directed) at the enemies of faith, the persecutors and executors of Christians.

Outpourings of vitriolic fervor are a part of the vision and psychology of a persecuted people, providing hope that their suffering is not the final word. If the Romans have come in the night and bashed my family to a pulp, I will want to know that their hate and destruction does not have the final word. If white slave owners come in the night and rape my children and set fire to my meager home, I will want to know that their hate and destruction does not have the final word (the language of the great African American spiritual tradition is one of the finest extra-biblical traditions of apocalyptic hope: "we shall not be moved"). If Hitler's brown-shirts come in the middle of the night and take me away for the sin of being Jewish or homosexual or an enemy of the state, I will want to know that their hate and destruction does not have the final word. Even, dare I say it, if Europeans come and declare my nation *terra nullius* and take away my language and my culture and hunt my people for sport, then I will want to know that their hate and destruction does not have the final word. This is language of hope for a people who have no hope. (I once knew an Anglican priest who intoned sonorously, "We pray that all people may have hope, especially those who have no hope." It was ponderous, but in a funny way it captured the heart of apocalyptic).

I write in an Australian context, but it is not atypical of any colonial context. Australian Christians should never forget that, while some missionaries spoke out against injustice to Australian Aboriginals, many did not, and the missionary methodology of many others was abhorrent even by the standards of the day. When one missionary, John Gribble, attempted to speak out on behalf of victimized Aboriginal people in Western Australia, the authorities in the Anglican Church sided with the moneyed pastoralists and removed his clerical license in an attempt to silence him. Although he died a near-broken man, he did establish a compassionate mission, at Yarabah in North Queensland, which continues to this day.[11]

Karl Marx would argue that this kind of hope, otherworldly hope, is the enemy of revolution, keeping peasants in their place and keeping

---

11. Harris, *One Blood*, 407–426, 497–500. See also Broome, *Aboriginal Australians*, 117–118.

corrupt governments in theirs. As it happens, bloody revolution has generally only ever bred more tyranny. As Alan Kreider once put it,

> in the French Revolution, a Mirabeau led inexorably to a Robespierre, who was after a short period of power forced to give way to the Directors. Ten years later France was ruled by an emperor, Napoleon I. Twenty years later another Bourbon was on the throne.[12]

In a similar context Julian Barnes observes drily, "At the start of the Revolution, Robespierre presided over the slaughter of priests; by its end, he was presiding over the slaughter of atheists."[13] Pendulums swing, however, and in the historical culture in which I am writing, when Christianity is coming to be seen as a social encumbrance, and the God of Christianity as "not great,"[14] it is likely that the priests of Christianity are once more at far more risk, if not of execution (in the West), then at least of social alienation and disdain. Apocalyptic revolutions often degenerate into indiscriminate slaughter, as the events of Bosnia-Herzegovina or Burundi and Rwanda reminded us in the 1980s and 1990s, and as the brutality of the killing fields of Syria reminds me as I write today. Christians, not especially, but also, will always be vulnerable: as I write a chilling video is circling the internet, recording in various degrees of detail the execution of a man who converted to Christianity in Tunisia. In Graham Greene's novel *The Power and the Glory*, the central character is a burned-out and alcoholic priest who stumbles to his own martyrdom at the hands of a dictatorship, too tired and confused to know whether or not he should continue to cling to the faith he has known, the faith that, while not a certainty in his life, is the only uncertainty that has become a habit and a source of comfort. While as a priest or as a Christian I hardly feel as vulnerable as this so-called whiskey priest, there is little doubt that the decency veneers of Western civilization are thin, so that as society's scorn turns on Christianity, its adherents, lay and ordained, may face immeasurable hatred in decades to come even in the nations that once were Christendom. At the same time they may continue to be perpetrators of evil—there have always been weeds among the wheat.[15] The reverberations of the feminist punk rock band Pussy Riot's media-sassy attack on the cozy relationship between Vladimir Putin and

---

12. Kreider, "Way of Christ," 54.
13. Barnes, *Nothing*, 82–83.
14. Hitchens, *God is Not Great*.
15. Matt 13:30.

the Patriarchy of Russian Orthodoxy should at the very least give cause for self-analytical concern within Christian communities.

Whether Karl Marx really wanted to eradicate Christianity as a religion of the oppressor, and whether it is a religion of the oppressor or not, are open to interpretation. If, however, this was essential to his social program, then he reckoned without a living God. While, as Kreider saw, revolution generally replaced one form of tyranny with another, God-filled apocalyptic vision has often brought about more lasting if still imperfect transitions: no outcome is the yet-to-come reign of God, but some of the great transitions have been beyond mere human imagining. The Roman Empire crumbled, and (for better or for worse) became Christendom. The evils of apartheid were overcome, and (for better or for worse) the African National Congress became the ruling party of South Africa. A black man, albeit not a descendant of southern US slaves, became (for better or for worse) the President of the US. But these are only signs along the way, and each is marred—as Christendom was, and South Africa and Obama surely are—by human sin and failure. The new heavens and new earth of Rev 21:1 (see also Isa 65:17, 66:22) will not be flawed: this is the hope of heaven.

Apocalyptic can only speak authentically, speak with the voice of God, when it is spoken from a position of powerlessness. The most apocalyptic statement in salvation history is the cry of Jesus on the cross, "it is finished" (John 19:30, repeated or at least alluded to in Rev 16:17 and 21:6). It is the precursor to the final and eternal vision of Rev 21. There needs to be no addition to the work achieved by Jesus in his powerless death at the hand of a corrupt state. In that moment "it is finished": God's transformation of despair into hope, darkness into light, Good Friday into Easter, corruption into "incorruption," is complete. It is finished.

However, in the hands of corrupt human beings, when they attain positions of power, the work of the Spirit is reversed. When apocalyptic is used by the state to force the conversion of Jews and Muslims (and others), the voice is no longer the true voice of apocalyptic. When apocalyptic is used by well-to-do and powerful Westerners to support the machinations of the militaristic State of Israel in its oppression of Palestinians, the voice is no longer the true voice of apocalyptic. When ecclesiastical hierarchies support unquestioningly the authority of (at the very least) a potentially corrupt Russian regime, then the apocalyptic edge of the church's voice is blunted beyond recognition; the feminist punks of Pussy Riot have highlighted this in Moscow. Three of their members (of a constantly fluid membership clearly designed far more for protest than for punk performances), Nadezhda Tolokonnikova, Maria Alyokhina and Yekaterina Samutsevich, were incarcerated, although Samutsevich has since been released on a suspended sentence, and they signify the battle against corruption from the inside of a Russian jail.

In our era of Western civilization, apocalyptic is more likely to be used by the spiritually bored as an occasionally lethal form of religious coercion. When foolish men like the American televangelist Harold Camping set out for a fourth (or fourteenth) time to predict the end of the world, they are removing the language of apocalyptic from its coordinates of suffering. Instead, they provide the coordinates of entertainment and sensationalism. At best they make fools of themselves. Often they rob gullible people of their possessions. At worst, as in the horrendous scenes of Waco Texas and Jonestown, Guyana, they become perpetrators of mass murder, generating tragedies that take on the darkest hues of the popular meaning of apocalypse. A group such as Brian Tamaki's Destiny Church in New Zealand needs to be watched closely, as it too appears to remove its apocalyptic language and praxis from the coordinates of suffering and powerlessness.[16] Apocalyptic, removed from these coordinates, can be a lethal weapon. It is our task to read it in its original context as a bringer of hope to the suffering and near-broken people of God.

Having said that, it must also be noted that the book of Revelation is not written to be read only by the oppressed in contexts of persecution. Even in its own time this was not the case. Christopher Rowland notes

> Revelation is not directed only to the persecuted. Several of the letters to the angels of the churches indicate that it is the comfortable who are being addressed, too. It is however more readily comprehended by those who, when they pray for God's reign to come on earth as in heaven, know that they live in Babylon and cannot be at ease with its habits and demands.[17]

Reading Revelation

The Bible is meant to be read aloud. Literacy, such as is enjoyed by most of us in the Western world, is a modern phenomenon. Literacy and printing

---

16. Vrankovitch, "Destiny Church."
17. Rowland, "Revelation," 569.

were driven by the Reformers and their immediate predecessors in faith, who saw that it was critical that interpretation of the Bible be removed from the hands of a select and often rather remote, biased and controlling "few" and put into the hands of all believers. It may well be asked if it is not necessary once again to liberate interpretation (or "hermeneutics") from the control of those with vested interests. Today the context is, at least on the surface, very different. The question remains the same: "who has the 'right' to determine correct interpretation of a text?" The players, however, are different. It is not the magisterium of the Roman Catholic Church that has exercised control over textual interpretation. Instead, as those who attempt to exercise hermeneutical individuality over formative texts in fiercely evangelical cultures soon discover, those with teaching and leadership ministries within many individual Protestant congregations exercise control over the interpretations permitted. It is a brave person, for example, who in many of these contexts, stands up and suggests that traditional teachings on sexuality or gender roles may be open to revision. It is a brave person who reminds the leadership of such contexts that Jesus has far more to say about dollars and cents than about human sexuality.

Perhaps the Reformers' process went too far. Many biblical texts are, as feminist theologian Phyllis Trible once put it in another context, "texts of terror."[18] They can be used to subject oppressed groups within the church to the will of controlling interests. In the "evangelical" wing of the Anglican Church, women were barred from ordination on the basis of a handful of texts about silence in church and submission to husbands—some women were forced to remain in abusive marriages, and children in abusive households, on the basis of the "submission texts" (Eph 5, Col 3). Some Anglican Church leaders, generally representing a more "Anglo-Catholic" wing of Anglicanism, alternatively argued that women could not be ordained because Jesus did not appoint female apostles. Homosexual people are barred from roles or even a place in some church communities on the basis of a handful of texts, interpreted in a particular way (e.g., Rom 1:26–27). Jewish people were oppressed and persecuted on the basis of a handful of texts and events in the Christian Scriptures (e.g., John 5:18). Texts can bring hope to oppressed people when interpretation is placed in their hands, and oppressed people around the world have learned to take strength from the narrative of God's people delivered from slavery. Slave owners saw the same texts in a very different way! How do we read the Bible?

---

18. Trible, *Texts of Terror*.

Babylon's Cap

There is another danger, most recently apparent in the ridiculous antics of Harold Camping referred to above. Fourteen times now, some say, and publically no fewer than four times, Camping has used his own bizarre interpretations of apocalyptic texts to predict the end of the world. He has claimed for himself absolute authority for his own interpretations of these texts, and he has convinced those who have followed his idiosyncratic interpretations that these alone are the authentic word of God. This could be laughable, but there is a sinister side to such idiocies, as those who fall for the rhetoric often sell up their goods (usually to the benefit of the false prophet) and await the Second Coming. The problems with Camping's form of biblical interpretation are myriad, but foremost among them is a fundamental misunderstanding. Prophecy, and the prophetic tradition in its biblical form, is not clairvoyance or crystal-ball gazing (see Rev 19:10). Prophesy, in its biblical form, is about interpretation of the present in the light of God's promised future. Walter Brueggeman says, "The task of the prophetic ministry is to nurture, nourish and evoke a consciousness and perception alternative to the consciousness and perception of the dominant culture around us."[19] Apocalyptic is a subset of prophesy, and it, too, is not concerned with gazing into a crystal ball, foreseeing which pope or politician is the antichrist. That is what Cullmann referred to above as "descriptions of the future which serve as pure speculations merely to serve human curiosity."[20] Of course, for those who do not have to put up with the harsh realities of oppression and suffering, crystal-ball gazing is "sexy" and exciting—and provides the interpreter with power and authority they would never otherwise have.

It was ever thus: in the second century a presbyter (= priest) named Montanus observed that the charismatic experiences and heroic sufferings of the earliest Christians were being absorbed into an ordered, structured and therefore allegedly "spiritless" church, and he began to redress the perceived problem by emphasizing spiritual and ecstatic gifts, along with predictions of the imminent return of Jesus. One scholar observed, "the explanation of the origins of Montanism lies in the fact that when the apocalyptic vision became less vivid and the church's polity more rigid, the extraordinary operations of the Spirit characteristic of the early church diminishes in both frequency and intensity."[21] Church rigidity was not, in

---

19. Brueggemann, *Prophetic Imagination*, 13.
20. Cullman, *Salvation*, 80.
21. Pelikan, *Emergence*, 98.

An Introduction to Apocalyptic

the view of Montanus, the dwelling place of God's Spirit. The birth and rebirth of apocalyptic and indeed pentecostal/charismatic movements ever since has followed this pattern, arising from and reacting against a rigid and sometimes stultifying church order as is often found, at the very least superficially, in traditional churches.

Montanus and his principal prophets (two women named Prisca and Maximilla) claimed to have direct illumination by God's Spirit or *Paraclete*. Thus illumined Montanus led his followers to the countryside of Phrygia (in modern terms central Anatolia, in Turkey) to await the Second Coming. He claimed that the mountain on which John of Patmos received his vision of the coming heavenly Jerusalem (Rev 21:10) was in Phrygia: what better place to await the *parousia* (Second Coming)? Montanus drifts away into the fictions of vitriolic biographers of the period: while it is not known what became of him or the key women who surrounded him, his opponents wrote lurid descriptions of their alleged suicide pact in order to discredit him.

In more recent decades, flamboyant figures, some basing their teachings on the writings of John of Patmos, have led themselves and their followers to cataclysmic deaths. Jim Jones, perpetrator of the unparalleled Jonestown massacre in 1978, was not in any orthodox sense a Christian, though he adopted sections of the apocalyptically influenced writings of the book of Acts to justify some of his teachings, particularly his seizure of the property of his followers. David Koresh, who died in what was effectively and controversially an act of "death by cop" when the Federal Bureau of Investigation burned his Branch Davidian compound to the ground in 1993, based his teachings more specifically on the book of Revelation. In each of these cases—Montanus, Jones, Koresh, Camping—and in countless more, a gross distortion of apocalyptic and its message of hope has taken place, resulting in various degrees of tragedy and abuse.

This was not what Phyllis Trible meant by a "text of terror"—she was referring to texts that dismantled self-interested power structures—but there is a connection. When an apocalyptic text is used by a person in a position of power to oppress or manipulate others—as in the case of Montanus, Jones, Koresh, and Camping—the outcome can be cataclysmic. Yet when people in a position of powerlessness use the language of apocalyptic, evil can be overcome. Martin Luther King was deeply influenced by the language of apocalyptic in general, and by the book of Revelation in particular. The future-apocalyptic dimensions of his "I have a dream" speech reached far beyond the possibility, now realized, of a black president. Those dimensions reach even beyond King's crescendo of optimism:

> When we let freedom ring, when we let it ring from every village and every hamlet, from every state and every city, we will be able to speed up that day when all of God's children, black men and white men, Jews and Gentiles, Protestants and Catholics, will be able to join hands and sing in the words of the old Negro spiritual, "Free at last! Free at last! Thank God Almighty, we are free at last!"

That vision of freedom in its human dimension must never be lost. If we lose that, in using the language of apocalyptic, then all we do have is pie in the sky. At the same time, apocalyptic, in its biblical forms, was never just about a social revolution: apocalyptic will always speak of a New Jerusalem, as yet unseen and even unimagined. To this extent Martin Luther King's apocalyptic vision is vastly different, polar, indeed, to John Lennon's "imagine there's no heaven." Paul of Tarsus, no less than John of Patmos, was using the language of apocalyptic when he broke out in ecstatic quotation "no eye has seen, nor ear heard, nor the human heart conceived, what God has prepared for those who love him" (1 Cor 2:9). So was Isaiah, when he wrote, long before John, of a new heavens and earth (Isa 65). This not merely about the occupancy of the White House!

To return then to my question, how *do* we read this book or any apocalyptic writing, how *do* we allow it to speak to us of God, but not to become an invitation to abuse or, at worse, cataclysm? How do we do this especially when most of us have never suffered for our faith, nor have most of us suffered economic or physical hardship on the base of our place in the hierarchies of society? We must never remove apocalyptic from its primary coordinates: God has compassion on the broken and disempowered. God's love and victory takes the shape not of a sword, but of a cross. We must always, in reading any biblical text, remember the circumstances of those who first wrote and heard the text. They were not generally practitioners of a powerful and respected religion, or wielders of authority in society, but were oppressed or at least alienated citizens of a hostile or at best indifferent world. They were the African American slaves of ancient centuries, not the slave owners. They were the potential victims at the wrong end of the muzzles of European hunters' guns, not the hunters.

At a more simple level, the answer to my question is: "out loud." The book of Revelation was a circular letter designed to be read aloud in the congregations named in its own chapters 2 and 3—or perhaps throughout

An Introduction to Apocalyptic

the emerging Christian network, of which those seven congregations were symbolic representatives. To read it out loud, or indeed at all, I recommend an easy to comprehend translation: I usually suggest the New Revised Standard Version as the appropriate version for liturgical and academic reading, and will be using it throughout this study. It is the ecumenically recognized standard for biblical study for those without biblical languages. But the demands of academic scholarship and the demands of aural absorption are not always the same. John of Patmos never wrote his vision as an academic exercise, and, while we could argue that it was written to be heard in a liturgical context, I doubt that the liturgies of Ephesus, Smyrna, Pergamum, Thyatira, Sardis, Philadelphia, and Laodicea had quite reached the aesthetic heights and exactitude of the contemporary liturgical churches! Perhaps we might hold two Bibles in our hands (or on our knees): the Contemporary English Version for ease of understanding and simplicity of reading, and the New Revised Standard Version as a basis on which to cross-check the translation. In the end the exact choice will remain yours; grab a version that you like, tip toe away into a room or a garden by yourself, and read it out aloud, chapter by chapter. The whole book of Revelation will only take about two hours to read—the tiny slices of Scripture we use in contemporary worship would have appeared strange to our forebears, who allowed far more time for worship than we do today. Read Revelation aloud,[22] and allow it to reverberate around; this is a poetic vision deep from the heart and the spirit of a man of God. Remember, too, that the author is a mere mortal, struggling with words to convey a vision beyond words: "the writer struggles to expand the boundaries of language to encapsulate what defies description"[23]—it is worth noting the number of times John uses the approximation "as if/like" (e.g., Rev 2:18). It is a problem for all biblical writers when they attempt to express the infinities of God and God's future.

For the remainder of this study we will divide the book into sections of a handful of chapters each. I do recommend that if you take my advice and read the book aloud to yourself, do so in segments of this size. Do not allow yourself to become bogged down in the sometimes quite macabre imagery. John was using language of a particular style and intensity to convey his vision—language that he and his audience had in common, which

---

22. Eugene Boring makes a similar observation; commenting on Rev 12, he stresses "The impact of the surrealistic drama communicated in chapters 12—14 comes not ny analysing it, but by hearing it read, or reading it, with imagination and insight." Boring, *Revelation*, 149.

23. Rowland, "Revelation," 560.

possible interceptors of the letter would not necessarily immediately comprehend. I am reminded of a billboard I once saw in Melbourne, Australia: "Demons slaughter Saints." Had I just arrived from John's Patmos, I may have been abysmally disturbed. As it happens, though, the words convey a different meaning in that Australian Rules Football-mad city. Other cultures will exercise similar shorthand: "Canes thrash Sharks" (I could only wish!) means much in southern hemisphere rugby union circles, but it is near-meaningless to anyone else. "Chiefs eat Kings" . . . the list of possibilities is endless, each specific to a code and a region.

So in the studies that follow I suggest you grab your simple English edition of the Bible, read out loud the chapters to be studied, and then begin to imagine how you might feel if you had been the original audience. They were gathering in households with brothers and sisters in Christ, isolated and frightened because of persecution, knowing that the wrath of the Roman Empire was building in antagonism towards them. Imagine you and I are with them, and that the fury of Roman power, towering like a Top End storm cloud (I write from Darwin, but a reader in, for example, Louisiana would relate to the imagery even if the terminology differs), stands tall over your household, your life and the life of your loved ones. What do the texts tell you about who is in control? What do the texts tell you about your future—and for that matter, the future of those who are threatening your life and the lives of your loved ones? Despite the storm clouds all around you, what do the texts tell you about who is in control, and who will have the final say?

Chapters and verses were a late addition to the biblical texts, and sometimes the divisions were a little arbitrary. But, roughly speaking, we will divide the twenty-two chapters of the book of Revelation into portions of four or five, and, to borrow a phrase, "break open the word" in that way. I will make no attempt at a verse-by-verse commentary—far better scholars than I have done that. As I make comments I will attempt to allow the text to speak meaningfully for your life in Australia or New Zealand or the US or Britain in the early twenty-first century. I will not however, draw Hal Lindsay-style—or Harold Camping-style—connections between the world of John of Patmos and our own, as if John were speaking about twenty-first century events. I hope we shall be drawn closer to the One in whom we believe all life has meaning and all centuries have meaning. As I write I will be bearing in mind those wonderful words of Martin Luther, who captured the essence of the book of Revelation in a hymn non-Lutherans sing too rarely, "A Safe Stronghold":

> A safe stronghold our God is still,
> a trusty shield and weapon;
> he'll keep us clear from all the ill
> that hath us now o'ertaken.

I may tread on some toes as we journey through John's extended vision, and may certainly, if I may slaughter a metaphor, ruffle the feathers of a few sacred cows.[24] Hopefully though, we may all be drawn closer through these studies to the One whom we celebrate each Easter dawn, the Alpha and Omega, the One who beckons "Come" (Rev 22:17).

---

24. The inter-testamental book 1 Enoch, which influenced or shared influences with John, refers to "a snow-white cow . . . with huge horns" (1 En 90:37). See Charlesworth, *Apocalyptic*, 71. The figure is a little like the sheaf of corn of Joseph's dream, to which the other sheaves must bow (Gen 37:7).

2

Write This Down! The Letters to the Churches (Revelation 1:1—3:22)

THE AUTHOR

THE NEW TESTAMENT WRITERS did not share our post-modern fascination with identity. We know a little about Luke and nothing about Matthew, Mark, or the John of the Fourth Gospel and epistles. The author of Hebrews is utterly anonymous, the epistles bearing the names of Peter and James are not definitely written by those New Testament figures, and Paul, while clearly identifiable, may not have written all the epistles attributed to him. Perhaps it is Paul, though, who provides the clue as to why these New Testament writers are so elusive: "It is no longer I who live, but it is Christ who lives in me," he tells the Galatians (Gal 2:20). This was no passing sentimental or pious comment, but a genuine belief that selfhood ceases to matter as we are absorbed into the Christ who redeems us, the Savior who enters our lives and transforms them from earthbound to "heaven-bound." At any rate, writing in the name and "authority" of another person was a widespread and honorable practice in the first century, and many of our New Testament documents stand in that tradition.

Our John does name himself (Rev 1:1, 4; 1:9), and he appears as a character in his narrative, but he is not interested in the details of his own biography. From the earliest decades of Christian history, the author of Revelation has been associated with the author of the Fourth Gospel and epistles. That author never names himself, referring to himself in the epistles as "the elder"

Write This Down! The Letters to the Churches (Revelation 1:1—3:22)

(2 John 1, 3 John 1) and, in the Gospel, elusively, as "the disciple who is testifying to these things" (John 21:24). We can surmise little more than that he was particularly close to Jesus, perhaps the "beloved disciple" that he refers to in his Jesus-story,[1] often present at key moments in Jesus' ministry. This figure does not always seem to coincide with the John of "James and John" (Mark 5:37), who seems incoherent in his ability to understand Jesus (Mark 10:35). Still, perspective is everything, and some thirty years had passed between the writing of the gospels and the events that they describe.

Perhaps the riddle of the identity of the gospel author John will escape us, this side of the *eschaton*. The question of our apocalyptic author's identity serves only to muddy the waters still more. From the second century onwards, debates have raged over the question of the authorship and authorial relationships between the documents bearing the name "John." Perhaps it was no more than a coincidence of names (assumed or genuine) that led to the link between the book of Revelation and the writings attributed to the disciple John. Perhaps there was a "school," a group of figures known or unknown to one another, but influenced by the apostolic John. Perhaps, in keeping with common practice in the ancient world, the author of Revelation adopted a name that associated him with a gospels-character, giving apostolic authority (imprimatur) to his often stern, always hope-filled message. Numerous, but not all contemporary scholars propose that the John of the Fourth Gospel and 1, 2, and 3 John is a different figure to the John of the book of Revelation.[2] I am not convinced we can be certain. The very fact that our author names himself in the opening sentences is, however, far removed from the elusive style of "the disciple who is testifying to these things" of the Fourth Gospel. Furthermore, our John's self-consciously apocalyptic style is often far removed from the "differently sophisticated" theological interpretations of the author of the Fourth Gospel—often, but not always: at the very least there seems to be a degree of influence of one document on the other.

Whatever we decide, both (if they are more than one) Johns reveal an utterly unshakeable belief in the Christ who is "the first and the last," as the apocalyptic John puts it, or was "in the beginning . . . with God" as the Fourth Gospel author puts it. Both are uninterested in speaking of themselves, because this eternal Christ, often pictured as "the Lamb" in Revelation (but see also John 1:29, 36), is the subject of the narrative, not John.

---

1. John 13:23, 19:26, 20:2, 21:7, 21:20.
2. For an alternative view and argument see Rowland, "Revelation," 514–17.

Babylon's Cap

A VISION? ¿QUÉ?

If you recall Manuel from the BBC comedy *Fawlty Towers*, you will probably recall the Spanish expression ¿*Qué?* (in Spanish, question marks enclose the question), spoken with furrowed eyebrows and uplifted palms. It is the way I feel when I am faced with conversations about the integrity and role of visions. For many years, in charismatic circles, I felt woefully inadequate, as fellow travelers spoke of their visions of and from God, or indeed spoke of God "speaking" to them. To this day I have no idea what this means. For many years I responded by dismissing the language as empty religious vernacular, a kind of religio-speak, religious language for "I thought," "I discovered," or "I decided." Certainly that is in broad terms the approach of scholars of religious language, such as the great Ian Ramsey[3] or my erstwhile teacher Peter Donovan, who emphasize that when religious people speak of their experiences they use conventions acceptable and understood within their group, but bewildering to outsiders.[4] What *does* Paul mean when he tells the Corinthians "I know a person in Christ who fourteen years ago was caught up to the third heaven" (2 Cor 12:2)? What *does* Mark mean when he recounts that Jesus saw the "heavens torn apart" (copied but subtly altered by Luke and Matthew) at his baptism (Mark 1.10)?

Yet in recent years, after more exposure to the deep wisdom of non-European traditions (not least Māori and Indigenous Australian traditions), I am less prepared to be dogmatic. Do people see visions like I see a movie? I do not know. Do people hear God's voice like I hear a telephone voice? I do not know. It is not my experience. What then John really means when he uses constructions such as "in the spirit" or "I heard behind me a loud voice like a trumpet" (Rev 1:10) I do not know. There are warnings here against too literal an interpretation—voices are not like a trumpet, any more than they are like a piano or tympani. This is a simile designed to jar, effectively designed not to work in any literal sense. A simile will always only draw comparisons, not exactitudes, but this one draws an impossible connection. To run like a hare, or like the wind, might make sense as an allusion to silent speed. However, while a trumpet is loud and piercing, it is not "like a voice." Most people who have moved in theological circles have heard many sniggers about the book of Revelation, John, and too many sacred mushrooms, but this is no random and undisciplined leap of an altered

---

3. Ramsey, *Religious Language*.
4. Donovan, *Religious Language*.

Write This Down! The Letters to the Churches (Revelation 1:1—3:22)

consciousness. John is warning us that this trumpet-sound belongs to an utterly unfamiliar, utterly *other* dimension, beyond our comprehension.

I would criticize those who speak of visions, even those who speak of surreal and disconnected visions, cautiously. Drug users, sufferers of epilepsy, and practitioners of intense mysticism will all speak of forms of synesthesia, by which senses become (if I may borrow a favorite "coined" word) "intertwingled," and the visionary may taste sound, hear scent, feel sight, and so on. T. S. Eliot, a visionary but not known as a user of mind-altering substances, provides an example in his early poem "Rhapsody on a Windy Night": "Every street-lamp that I pass / Beats like a fatalistic drum"; even in the days of gaslight, streetlights were not famous for a drum-like sound.[5] William James writes of his own experimentations with nitrous oxide leading to a state in which "the opposites of the world, whose contradictoriness and conflict make all our difficulties and troubles, were melted into unity."[6] Psychiatrists may be able to tell us about the synapses of the complex human brain, but I suspect that will not help us understand the book of Revelation. Was John carried, perhaps in a time of intense prayer (it was on the Lord's Day—Rev 1:10), into an ecstatic state? It is highly possible. Christopher Rowland urges us to err on the side of respect for our author:

> We know little other than what the book tells us about how John received this revelation. We will never know whether, like a poet, he exercised that mixture of imagination and attention to form that is characteristic of poetry, or whether he offers in the book the account of a true visionary experience. Many commentators suppose that Revelation is an attempt to write an apocalypse, much as Paul would have written an epistle. Such an assessment is unsatisfactory, however. There are signs in the book of that dream-like quality in which the visionary not only sees but also is involved (e.g., 1:12, 17; 5:4; 7:13; 11:1; 17:3; c.f. 1:10, 21:10). We should pay John the compliment of accepting his claim—unless we find strong reasons for denying it.[7]

It is however safe to say that, however he gained his insight, John crafted it carefully to maximize its potential to convey meaning to his audiences, using symbols and tools and styles (often called "conventions"), to ensure they had every opportunity to "listen to what the Spirit is saying to the

---

5. Brown, "T. S. Eliot," 493.
6. William James, cited by Wilson, *Reasons*, 34.
7. Rowland, "Revelation," 514.

churches".[8] John received a vision, but he worked very hard to craft it in terms intelligible to his audiences. He did so in response to the command "write" (Rev 1:11, 1:19, and throughout the book).

THE CHURCH OR THE CHURCHES?

The idea of a single, universal church, while a profound insight into the nature of the Body of Christ (as Paul preferred to see it), is a post-New Testament concept. When the *New Zealand Anglican Prayer Book / He Karakia Mihinare o Aotearoa* uses the phrase "Hear what the Spirit is saying to the church" as a liturgical response at the end of the Old Testament and Epistle readings in the Eucharist, it has altered John's words. To change the word "churches" to "the church" (even with the old-style capitalized "C" as used in the New Zealand book) is to make a theological statement foreign to John, and we should not impose it on or read it into his text. We should not impose a later view of the "church" as a universal, "catholic" body, onto a New Testament text. It may be right for us to see the world in this way in the global village of the twenty first century, for by the time of the Great Councils, the Church Fathers were speaking of "one holy catholic and apostolic church," And their insight was a profound one. But this language is not John's language. The "churches" of which he speaks were gathered congregations. The Reformers reclaimed the notion of individual churches at the time of the Reformation, and did so in an attempt to re-impose a strictly biblical world view on the Christian communities. Whether they were right to do this is an entirely different matter.

As it happens, I believe the Protestant Reformers were wrong to try to set the clock back, but it has to be acknowledged they had our author on their side. Unlike the Fathers of the Great Councils, our John did not have the benefit of three centuries of theological reflection in and on the Spirit. To John, the gathered congregations, the "churches," were the place where the Spirit spoke. The Spirit links John's century, the Church Fathers' centuries, the Reformers' centuries, and our own century: the Spirit is not static, and individuals and institutions guided by the Spirit grow into new self-understandings; by the fourth century the church was seen in a different way. For the purposes of these studies, I will follow John's lead, and the churches will be the congregations.

---

8. Rev 2:7, 2:11, 2:17, 2:29, 3:6, 3:13, 3:22.

Write This Down! The Letters to the Churches (Revelation 1:1—3:22)

TO WHOM?

John did not write for us. He wrote for "the seven churches that are in Asia." In the light of what has just been said, we might translate that as "the seven congregations that were in Asia." It is estimated that the congregations to which Paul wrote his letters were groups of some twenty-five to thirty-five people, gathering as house churches in the homes of some of the wealthier believers. We can fairly safely assume that little had changed by the time John was setting down his vision. Ephesus, named by John, was one of the communities well known to Paul (1 Cor 16:8), and it was the capital of the region known as "Asia," or technically "Asia Minor." It is a region far smaller than the regions covered by our use of the term "Asia," loosely covering the regions that today we would designate as northern and eastern Greece and southern Turkey. Apart from Ephesus, John names Smyrna, Pergamum, Thyatira, Sardis, Philadelphia, and Laodicea, forming a cluster of settlements on the Aegean coast and hinterland.

The book of Revelation is a "circular," a letter written to at least seven separate communities. Each would have heard the letter read aloud, each would have heard their own message—some warm and affectionate in encouragement and affirmation, some less so—and the message of their sibling believers elsewhere. John begins with the traditional formulae of letter writing, solemnly stating the authority and weight of the writing to follow (Paul often begins his letters with a statement of his authority). This opening flourish, however, makes a remarkable claim: the authority behind the writer is Jesus Christ himself (Rev 1:1). John would hardly have been able to make such a claim if his own credentials as a servant of Christ were questionable, the more so as he moves on to make the bold statement that he personally has been able to witness the vision he goes on to relate.[9]

In the light of my earlier comments on contemporary cults and their founders, it is worth noting that John moves on quickly from mentioning his own role, ensuring that the focus stays on the source of the revelation, Jesus. This revelation will not be about John, but about Jesus. John greets his audiences (Rev 1:4), but immediately conveys the greater greeting, "from Jesus Christ, the faithful witness, the firstborn of the dead, and the ruler of the kings of the earth." The chain of command is established.

---

9. This is so even if John himself was not entirely familiar with his audiences, as Aune suggests. See Aune, *Revelation 1–5*, xliv.

Babylon's Cap

How brave that claim is! From the very opening sentences, John, if not actually casting a gauntlet at the feet of Caesar, nevertheless makes sure it falls there. If not deliberately provocative, spoiling for a fight, this is still making a collision of claims likely. Caesar—who considers himself divine—is subject to the God of the crucified criminal Jesus Christ. The seven churches of Asia Minor (there were many more, including Troas, Colossae, and Hieropolis: perhaps in some way these seven were only representative, and John expected a wider audience) knew immediately that a fight was in the offing. Even lukewarm Laodicea would have nowhere to hide as the clash of imperial claims was orchestrated. Bauckham notes, "John sees that the nature of Roman power is such that, if Christians are faithful witnesses to God, then they must suffer the inevitable clash between Rome's divine pretensions and their witness to the true God."[10]

Once John has established that his God is "bigger" than Caesar, he then associates the crucified Christ as uniquely associated with, even related to God. The poetic acclamation of Rev 1:7 is no mere filler, but a daring association of Jesus with the visionary figures of Dan 7:13 and Zech 12:10. These are complex texts that at the very least speak of one who will suffer because of their unique preparedness to be and to do the will of God. The Zechariah text in particular influences the portrayal of Jesus in the Fourth Gospel (note especially John 19:37, where it is quoted directly), and its notion of "like a firstborn" soon shaped early Christian language of the relationship between Jesus and the one he calls *Abba*, Father.

Even more daring, John shifts immediately to speak of the incomparable nature and status of God: "I am the Alpha and the Omega". It would appear to be God who is referred to, but by Rev 21:5 and 22:12 something has shifted, and the separation of divine Father and divine Son is impossible (another echo of the Fourth Gospel: John 10:30, 17:11, 17:22). As the book of Revelation goes on we will find increasing if shadowy hints of a trinitarian understanding of God.

At this stage as John speaks of the Spirit, though, he prefers to use the unique construct "the seven spirits." We need to be cautious before ticking each spirit off on the fingers of our hands: John is self-consciously using the language of apocalyptic, and "seven" is a highly significant figure in apocalyptic discourse. Even in the older, pre-apocalyptic stories of Genesis we will see "sevens" appearing everywhere: seven days of creation in Gen 1:1—2.3, seven ewe lambs in Gen 21, seven years of service by Jacob in Gen 29, Jacob's

---

10. Bauckham, *Theology*, 38.

Write This Down! The Letters to the Churches (Revelation 1:1—3:22)

seven profound bows as he approaches Esau (Gen 31:3). In Gen 41 we find an impenetrable wall of sevens: seven sleek cows, seven emaciated cows, seven plump ears of grain, seven withered ears of grain, designating of course the seven years of plenty and the seven years of famine. It was these years of plenty and years of famine that established Joseph's greatness in Egypt. The same patterns appear in Exodus, Leviticus, Numbers, and Deuteronomy, not to mention in subsequent theological developments in the post-canonical church: seven deadly sins, seven virtues, seven sacraments.[11]

Sometimes a cigar is just a cigar, and seven simply means seven, but as the use of the number accumulates through the Pentateuch it begins to take on an almost mystical meaning (reflected in the question of forgiveness Peter puts to Jesus in Matt 18), a perfection or an infinity. In the book of Joshua, seven priests bear seven rams' horns and circle the city seven times. When Elisha resuscitates the child of the Shunammite woman the child sneezes seven times, and Naaman is told to wash seven times in the Jordan. The plethora of biblical sevens goes on, until its symbolic meaning, "a large number" (as several times in the book of Daniel, and perhaps Mt. 12.45), or indeed "a perfect number," dominates. The notion of infinity or perfection underscores the response of Jesus to Peter's question about the extent of forgiveness.

The number seven appears no fewer than fifty-five times in the book of Revelation. But in reading the numerology of Revelation we need not become silly. Sometimes John uses numbers in a faintly coded way, but this is not a study in occult (which simply means "secret") coding. I recall vividly the anticipation that swept millennialist circles in the late 1970s when it was realized that the Bankcard symbol, three superimposed b's, could be interpreted as three superimposed 6's.

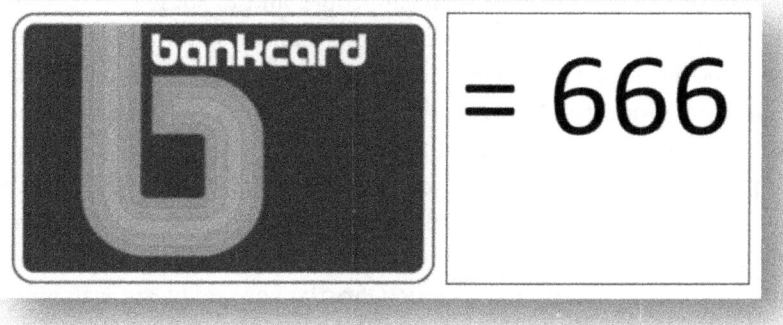

---

11. Pelikan, *Reformation*, 293.

Babylon's Cap

Was this the "mark of the beast" (Rev 13:16–17), the first step towards "one world government," the beginning of the End? Others added up (in various combinations) the numeric value (A=1, B=2, etc.) of the name of Henry Kissinger to reach 666, proving he was the Antichrist (allegedly Rev 13:18). I was in New Zealand at the time, and found a way (long since forgotten!) to demonstrate that that country's Prime Minister Robert Muldoon's name could be made to add up to 666; my ironic dismantling of the sensationalist millennialists' occult arguments was not appreciated.

John's original audience, however, had no doubt about the significance of "one world government." They lived under the aegis of Caesar, who held dictatorial sway over the known world. Seven hundred years earlier, the Hebrew people had experienced the same tyranny at the hands of Babylonian King Nebuchadnezzar (whose cap has given its name to this study; we will ask soon who wears this cap today). Long before John's audience, before the emergence of the language of apocalyptic, the Hebrew ancestors had known the tyrannical rule of Pharaoh.

Since biblical times, Christians have experienced totalitarianism in many guises. The victims of the Inquisition knew the totalitarian authority of emperor and pope. Protestants and Catholics alike came to know their opponents' totalitarian proclivities—it is no accident that the artist Albrecht Dürer, Roman Catholic but sympathetic to Luther, turned to the imagery of apocalyptic at the end of the fifteenth century. Although he himself avoided persecution, he witnessed some of the most tumultuous times in political history since Christ. (Soon even these events would be overshadowed as a cataclysmic plague swept, for at least the second time, across the face of Europe and the world, ended in Britain only by an equally cataclysmic fire.) Jews under Hitler, along with physically and intellectually handicapped people, homosexual people, and to some extent Roman Catholics, experienced the horror of totalitarianism; so too have Christians (and Jews) in the former Soviet Union or Communist China. Christians proclaiming God's rule of justice in apartheid South Africa experienced if not totalitarianism then at least the inescapable thuggery of the unmovable political machine. Anglican and other Christians in Robert Mugabe's Zimbabwe are at the time of writing experiencing similar victimization, and converts to Christianity in Tunisia are, according to internet memes, being tortured and executed. Coptic Christians in Egypt are watching in fear the possibility of new forms of totalitarianism and Sharia law. None of these corrupt governments is, technically, "one world government," though some have tried, but each has been the totality of government in the world available to and impacting on the lives of suffering believers.

Which brings us back to the seven spirits speaking to the seven churches. The seven spirits are—is, we might say with grammatical abandon—the one Spirit. We might even go so far as to say the seven churches were the one church; no doubt the letter of John was read aloud in Ephesus, Smyrna, Pergamum, Thyatira, Sardis, Philadelphia, and Laodicea, but it is likely it was intended by John to reach further than those actual and representative centers. The fact I am writing about it in Darwin two thousand years later suggests he was right. It seems the Fathers were right too, as they spoke of "one holy, catholic and apostolic church," the people of God throughout space and time.

WHY WRITE?

John writes primarily because he has been commanded to in his visionary experience. Perhaps then, if we ask "why" Revelation was written, we are asking the question not of John but of God. As we look at the content of the brief individualized congregational portions of the letter, the addresses to each of the seven churches (or, technically, to the "angels" or "messengers"—the word is the same—of each of the seven churches), we may see why the vision was narrated in the last decade of the first century and why it can and must still speak to us today.

Ephesus

John provides his first imprimatur or authentication of his vision, indicating that he has received special and privileged revelation from "one like the Son of Man" (the gospels apply this title to Jesus eighty-five times; it will appear again in Rev 14:14). He needs no further authentication—John was probably well known to his audiences—so he turns his attention to the church at Ephesus. Ephesus is a port city, a strategic city, and as we have noticed, a city closely linked with Paul. (There are disputes as to whether the Letter to the Ephesians was written by Paul, despite Eph 1:1; as noted above, to write in someone's name was quite a reputable practice in Paul's time, and there are some stylistic and theological differences when Ephesians is compared to his undisputed letters. First Corinthians was, however, written *from* Ephesus.) Ephesus was a comparatively wealthy city, and the Christian community may have reflected that. Somehow the church of Ephesus has, despite "patient endurance" (Rev 2:2), reneged or "fallen" (Rev 2:5) regarding the quality of its love.

The word here translated "patient endurance" (John applies the phrase to himself in Rev 1:9) is a quality much valued in the New Testament, not least by Luke when, in the explanation of the Parable of the Sower, he uses it as description of the merit of those who are "seed that falls on good soil" (see Luke 8:15). When Paul wrote to Corinth, from Ephesus, he had emphasized that there is a more important ingredient of Christian witness, "a more excellent way": the way of love (1 Cor 13). However, in Revelation, it appears that the searchlight of another prophet is now turned on the Ephesian faith community: "you have abandoned the love you had at first" (Rev 2:4). It may be that John was aware of the effect Paul's "Hymn to Love," written in Ephesus but sent to Corinth, had in the formation and instruction of the Ephesian Christians' faith. John's critique of the Ephesians' lovelessness is a biting one, coming as it does after sentences praising their tenacity, purity ("you cannot tolerate evildoers," "you have tested those who claim to be apostles"), and stamina. It is hard not to recall Paul's words: "without love . . . I am a noisy gong or a clanging cymbal . . . I am nothing . . . I gain nothing" (1 Cor 13:1–3). While it cannot be proved our author is probably making a direct allusion to Paul's words, those words were already likely to have been widely known around the Christian communities of Asia Minor by the time John wrote.

The message to the Ephesians warns that their "lampstand" (cf. Mark 4:21) will be taken from them if their lovelessness is not rectified. It is a timeless warning—the witness of any faith community becomes meaningless gibberish if love is absent, or exploitation and abuse present. We might remember with shame that the witness of the post-Constantine church has often been marred by lovelessness, and that we need to be very sure of ourselves indeed if we risk singing "they'll know we are Christians by our love." Will "they"? Did Roman Catholics executed by Protestants or vice versa know their opponents' faith by the quality of their love? Do victims of sexual and psychological abuse by church representatives "know we are Christians by our love"? Will those living in the impoverished and war-torn nations of the world today know that we are Christians by our love? As some of the members of Pussy Riot languish in a Russian jail, victimized by a cozy alliance of church and state, will they "know we are Christians by our love"? Many analysts have reminded us that 9/11 and the aggression of

Write This Down! The Letters to the Churches (Revelation 1:1—3:22)

militant Islam is at least in part related to, or fed by, Muslim observations of the gap between what they perceive to be the "Christian" global north and the state of many impoverished Islamic communities. This perspective is exacerbated by long-held memories of the Crusades in which Muslims, Jews and Orthodox Christians were slaughtered by the Christian crusaders. "They'll know we are Christians by our love." Will residents of nations threatened with the devastation caused by global warming—Christian nations among them—"know we are Christians by our love," as we respond with slothful progress to their plight and its causes? Will the peoples of West Papua, suffering cultural genocide at the hands of Indonesian authorities, "know we are Christians by our love," as we respond with resounding silence to their plight?

There are no clear answers to the questions I have asked above, or to any questions of the "who" of salvation: we have often claimed that biblical demands exclude practitioners of various forms of behavior from fellowship with Christ, and even John continues with a final, and to us now obscure, word of exclusion regarding the Nicolaitans (Rev 2:6). But we need to pursue our questions further still: will those whose sexuality bars them from full involvement in the life of the church "know we are Christians by our love"? If a person's behavior destroys believers' relationship with Christ—and this would seem to be the case of the "works of the Nicolaitans"—then there is room for censure and even exclusion (1 Cor 5:5, 1 Tim 1:20). Generally, however, this directive to censure and exclude implicates and condemns sexual predators (or exhibitionists, which in a strange way was the case at Corinth) rather than, for example, human beings living in faithful monogamous partnerships or mutually enriching love. The example I generally use is that of Nobel laureate Patrick White and his partner Manoly Lascaris: despite an epiphanous near-conversion experience, the prohibition of White's love for Lascaris, combined with the immeasurable silliness of a prohibition on guessing games involving the number of beans in a jar at a church fete, ensured that White was never able to practice his tentative faith as a part of the Anglican Church to which he once belonged.[12] Did White and Lascaris know that Sydney Anglicans were Christians by their love? There is no doubt about White's close proximity to Christian faith: he saw his novels as giving "professed unbelievers a glimpse of their own unprofessed faith,"[13] and described himself as, after

---

12. White, *Flaws in the Glass*, 144–45.
13. Cited by Wilson, *Reasons*, 25.

the beans in a jar event, having "retreated into his private faith," maintaining "inklings of God's presence."[14] By excluding him from its fellowship and sacraments, the Christian community failed to profess the quality of its love, and that in part contributed to White's lifetime yearning ambivalence to Christian faith.

We are not called to be a community of "anything goes," but a community of love. Apart from Jesus' very stern words of exclusion, by which many of us if not most of us would (were it not for grace) stand condemned (Matt 5:28, for any males amongst us? Matt 25:44, any of us?), there are few biblical references to exclusion or expulsion from the community of Christ. First Corinthians 5:5 and 2 Cor 2:1–9 are among the only clear references to exclusion from fellowship; neither is with reference to homosexuality, and the latter is clearly only a temporary exclusion, probably because someone has dared to oppose Paul's apostolic authority!

Smyrna

John then turns to the Smyrnans. Smyrna (modern Izmir) was also a prosperous port city. There are indications that there was considerable animosity between Jews and Christians in this city. Once more we need to be careful: the history of Christian attitudes to and treatment of the Jews is a blight on our history: can Jews "know we are Christians by our love?" Nevertheless Revelation was written, like the Fourth Gospel and indeed the First Gospel, at a time when the Jews were aggressive in their response to the new and aberrant religion growing in their midst.

They had good cause to be. Their relationship to Roman authority was uneasy, and not all wanted to spark a repetition of the events that led to destruction of their Second Temple some years before Revelation was written. Perhaps they had compromised in their relationship to Caesar. But we can hardly blame them: massacre is such an unattractive option, no matter how noble it may seem. The Romans on the other hand were not interested in differentiating between Jews and Christians, and the latter were causing trouble. As with any reading of Scripture, we must avoid finger pointing: it has not been unknown, however undesirable, for Christians to compromise in their relationship with the state—even to become the state in Constantine's questionable legacy to Christendom (achieved also by Israel since 1947, with similar consequences).

14. White, *Flaws in the Glass*, 145.

Write This Down! The Letters to the Churches (Revelation 1:1—3:22)

The context of the early Jesus-movement was one of great vulnerability, as many of the Christians worshiped as a part of synagogue communities and claimed to be the true descendants of Abraham. This was always going to end in tears, and the animosity between the religious (not necessarily racial) groups was soon creating times of trial for the Smyrnan people. Paul's letter to the Thessalonians reveals a similar context: in Thessalonica, Christians and their antagonism to the Lordship of Caesar were coming to the attention of authorities, Jewish and Roman alike, who were keen to keep "in" with Rome. The Thessalonian Christians, too, were ostracized: Paul uses the same word (*thlipsis*), often translated as "suffering(s)." It is the word used of the choked seed in Mark 4 and Matt 13, suggesting that those recorders of Jesus' words, and presumably Jesus himself, saw suffering as an inevitable corollary of following the Way of the Cross.

So John in his vision lashes out at "those who say that they are Jews and are not, but are a synagogue of Satan" (Rev 2:9). Commenting on John's words, Wilfrid Harrington comments dryly, "The sad overkill of polemic!"[15] We are treading on eggshells when we read an exclamation such as this after a two thousand year-history of Christian persecution of Jewish people. There is a tension here. It is tempting, when we are reading Revelation after the events of Auschwitz (where Auschwitz becomes not one death camp but a symbol of all anti-Jewish pogroms and persecutions), to excise these words. Yet, however unfortunate, however demonic, even, they may be (and dare we speak of a demonic passage in Scripture?), they are a part of our story as the Christ-following people of God. The stern warning that concludes the book of Revelation, Rev 22:9, must be taken seriously, and we cannot play games with the ancient texts of our faith. We cannot delete texts because our history has so abused them. They are often the *cries de cœur* of wounded hearts, and we cannot deny their pain—Ps 137:9 is the most chilling example of all. How then do we read them?

Who has not cried out in pain and anger, especially when at the receiving end of injustice? We well might want to wonder how many broken peoples today are still crying out, longing for justice and compassion at the hands of victors and oppressors. Post-Auschwitz, I am inclined to join the Paul of Romans, rather than the Paul of Galatians, recognizing that by the grace of God the God-fearing Jews, as well as God-fearing Gentiles, are to wear the sobriquet "People of God." Post *terra nullius*[16] I am tempted to say more:

---

15. Harrington, *Revelation*, 58.

16. This is the declaration in 1788 that Australia was an uninhabited land. A particularly potent discussion of the on-going issues involved is Merete Borch, "Rethinking."

while we applaud the bravery of those missionaries who stood in front of the muzzles of the hunters' guns, we must acknowledge that our "Christianized Europe" has done immeasurable evil, and that in the minds of many broken peoples, not least the anti-authoritarian feminist punk-rockers of Pussy Riot, that evil is inseparably linked with the Gospel of Jesus Christ. Might not our Aboriginal brothers and sisters have cried out to the effect of "they say they are Christians and are not, but are a synagogue of Satan?" (Rev 2:9).

The fact that *any* Indigenous people, here or elsewhere, believe "our" gospel at all is an act of enormous tenacity and graciousness on their part. That many do not is entirely understandable; we can only pray that, now Christians are increasingly a powerless minority in society, we will slowly transform into a faith-people whose actions speak to displaced and hurting races about a gracious Savior. We can only pray that, now we have no big sticks to wield, we will proclaim by our love a Savior who can still heal dysfunctional individuals and communities. Those Indigenous communities have an ancient narrative that has sometimes—often—been shattered by our near-genocidal intrusion. We can only pray that we proclaim by word and action a Savior who can reconcile racial and economic divides, forgiving even those who have oppressed and abused, and leading us all to a coming reign of justice and peace.

This, though, is a far cry from the position of the Christian community in Smyrna. They were not oppressors but oppressed. Their faith was causing them to be, like Jesus himself, handed over to suffer and die (Rev 2:10). John did not promise that this would not take place, that they would not die, because to follow Christ is not a protection from suffering. He promised them a different perspective, a different "narrative," in which their almost certainly painful deaths would lead to a crowning beyond comprehension in the story of God. In the terms of *A Beautiful Life* he offers them a German tank—but this prize which he calls "the crown of life" is far greater than a mere tank (or even a mere crown). Later in the book of Revelation John will present images of a hereafter beyond human words. As Bauckham observes, "It is not that the here-and-now are left behind in an escape into heaven or the eschatological future, but that the here-and-now look quite different when they are opened to transcendence."[17] The Smyrnan Christians receive an eschatological hope for which to live and die and live again.

---

17. Bauckham, *Theology*, 18.

Write This Down! The Letters to the Churches (Revelation 1:1—3:22)

Pergamum

The Christians of Pergamum faced an invidious situation, though they were not alone in the Christian communities in doing so. Pergamum was not a port city, being inland, some seventy kilometers north of Smyrna. It was however a strategic administrative city in the Roman Empire. Like many such cities, its populace received benefits from the emperor in return for carrying out his work—*and worshiping him*. Its citizenry consequently were not happy to find a small new religious sect in their midst, stirring up trouble with the emperor. The Christians could possibly have compromised, adopting a form of syncretistic religion by which they worshipped Christ and Caesar, but this was not the path to which the prophets, not least Jesus (e.g., Matt 6:24), called them (then or now). Compromise and syncretism was not the heritage of the three men of the furnace in Daniel. The words of Joshua "choose this day whom you will serve" (Josh 24:15) have reverberated through Christian and Jewish history, and, despite the arguably good intention of many syncretistic theologians and missionaries,[18] it is doubtful that a merger of religious truths has any imprimatur in our history.

The Christians of Pergamum have done well, holding fast to their faith without compromise, even when one of their number was executed for his faith (Rev 2:13). But an issue has arisen (not for the first time in the short history of the Christian community: see 1 Cor 8) regarding the consumption of food offered to idols. This was no simple matter for the early Christians: it was as if a Western nation's supermarkets and butchers, with a near monopoly on meat sales, sold meat only after it had been offered in rituals to a national deity. Would we purchase and eat it? The arguments are all there in 1 Corinthians: "what does it matter—idols are not real because there is only one God." "Sure—but what if our sisters and brothers have in the past been influenced and controlled by the idols, and still, despite release, fear their influence? Is it right then to eat meat that has been sacrificed to them—even if it is the only meat available?"

These are not merely historical issues and are not merely about food: Indigenous people in Australia have to wrestle with these questions in the context of ancient rites and ceremonies. Missionaries from evangelical traditions took a hard line: the rites and ceremonies of the Dreaming, for example, by which the ancient Australian Aboriginal Dreamtime is made present again, were seen as belonging to a pre-Christian and therefore pagan past. W. E. H.

---

18. I think in particular of John Hick and Raimundo Pannikar.

Stanner tellingly observed, "many customs, in themselves not only innocent of evil or repugnant elements but, in fact, of a sacramental order, were ... suppressed by missionaries."[19] Was there a "more excellent way"? Is there still?

The "pagan past" was emphasized when the word "dreaming" was used relatively recently in the Kriol Bible[20] to translate the Hebrew notion of idols and false gods: was all observation of a Dreaming ceremony to be seen as idolatrous or demonic? Margaret Micken, coordinator of the Kriol Bible translation team, was interviewed about the use of the word on the ABC Radio National's *Religion Report*. When Noel Debien asked "You've used the word 'dreaming' as that which is to be rejected?" Micken responded at length:

> Aboriginal people are also on a journey of understanding their culture and understanding what in their culture they're able to retain, and so it becomes a very complex thing. But in the end, after much discussion, they all agreed, the translation team agreed to retain that terminology, because it is something that still has impact. But some of them are now separating out the dreaming type issues in their culture, and just calling something that's just their cultural things that they do. So for example, the relationships are still cultural things that they can participate in. Some have not been participating in particular ceremonies because they don't feel it's right to do that. And so they're on a journey actually really working out how does this all fit together, how does God's word, what does God's word say to them in Kriol, and of course because they can understand it more clearly, I think it's more of a challenge for them.[21]

If we dig deep into the meaning of "Dreaming" in this Aboriginal context, we can see that it is not a simple and perhaps paternalistic matter of throwing out all that is ancient in a culture, but of allowing members of a culture themselves to discover what is and what is not consistent with the service of the gospel, the way of Jesus Christ. Micken refers to "separating out the dreaming type issues in their culture, and just calling something that's just

---

19. Stanner, *White Man*, 140.

20. Kriol is a modern "Europeanised" Aboriginal language designed to facilitate communication between Aboriginal and European peoples. There were hundreds of Aboriginal languages across pre-colonial Australia, many now irretrievably lost. Kriol, like Swahili in north-east Africa, or "Pidgin" in Papua New Guinea, is not universally accepted amongst Aboriginal peoples, and is considered by many to be a paternalistic imposition.

21. Debien, "First Complete Bible Translation," Paragraph 14.

their cultural things that they do." If aspects of a culture detract from the centrality of what Paul calls "Christ and him crucified" (1 Cor 2:2)—in Corinth and Pergamum it is apparent that eating idol-offered meat was such an aspect—then it is to be jettisoned. We might assume that Pacific or Incan ritual cannibalism might fall into the same category. On the other hand, when allegedly "ritualized acts of sex" were interpreted as evidence that Australian Aboriginals were "men of Sodom, sinners exceedingly," even though the rituals were enactments of non-sexual life experiences, it was unlikely to foster cross-cultural understanding and respect.[22]

> The suppressors did not suspect that they themselves were trying to impose a symbolism which had only an historical, and not an essential, connection with the deeper metaphysical truths of their faith. But it was a blindness of the mind's eye, not just poor observation or lack of information, that made the ritual uses of water, blood, earth, and other substances, in combination with words, gestures, chants, songs, and dances, all having for Aborigines a compelling authority, appear to Europeans mere barbarisms without sacramental authority.[23]

It is not for me to say what in the Dreaming is and is not consistent with following Jesus Christ, and as a European I would need to be very careful in doing so: Christian missionaries soon found it expedient to adopt pagan feasts of the northern hemisphere, solstices and equinoxes, as vehicles of the liturgical calendar (and that despite Paul's expressed horror in Gal 4:10). It is for me to proclaim "Christ and him crucified" and to entrust those who have received that proclamation to discern for themselves what in their relationship with Christ is and is not detrimental to their faith journey. I choose to drink alcohol, but would not do so in a context where those around me might be thwarted in their attempt to follow Jesus. Some Corinthian Christians may have continued to eat idol-offered meat (though I suspect Paul did not *really* like them doing so), but ceased to do so when others were around who might stumble in faith when caused to do likewise. There are even credible arguments for jettisoning calendrical feasts—the Closed Brethren do so—though I vehemently continue to uphold their value.

Dreaming? It is not for me to say, although I suspect with time (maybe centuries) Aboriginal Christians will visit and revisit the questions of what to retain and what to reject from their ancient traditions. Translators of the Bible into the Māori language, incidentally, rejected the name Io, who

22. Stanner, *White Man*, 140.
23. Ibid., 141.

is the creator god in Māori mythology, in favor of the generic divine name "Atua." Christians in Muslim cultures have wrestled and are wrestling again with the word "Allah." Like Paul, I would in all things urge on the side of caution: Matt 18:6 is a stern admonition, delivering a deeply threatening message to those who would put "stumbling blocks" in the way of children, and probably in the way of all childlike faith: it is not a Jesus-saying to be trivialized. Words are carriers of great significance, and we must use them with great caution. I would be very critical of any follower of Christ who dismissed the deep wisdom that is present in many aspects of Australian and other Indigenous communities, but words, too, may generate collateral damage. We need to speak of our faith with an ear open to the way it may sound to others.

Perhaps C. S. Lewis is hinting at the same when he has Aslan tell the children

> [T]hough the witch knew the Deep Magic, there is a magic deeper still which she did not know. Her knowledge goes back only to the dawn of time. But if she could have looked a little further back, into the stillness and the darkness before Time dawned, she would have read there a deeper incantation.[24]

Lewis is referring to the mysteries of salvation, and I would not want to suggest that the Dreaming is salvation. But it is vastly ancient, and its adherents lived by it for countless centuries before the missionaries came: Jesus said "I have other sheep that do not belong to this fold" (John 10:16), after all.

This may all seem far removed from Pergamum, but is it? John too refers to "causing others to stumble" (see Rev 2:14), and the message for those that do so is no less stern than that of Jesus: "I will come to you soon and make war against them with the sword of my mouth" (Rev 2:16). There is nothing syncretistic about this, no room for compromise with the gods or even the living standards of Roman society. And "fornication," this apparent example of "barbarism without sacramental authority," as Stanner put it? In reality, despite the missionaries' fears, this is probably not what the Indigenous dancers were doing, for strict rules governed Indigenous sexual relations: there was a fundamental breakdown in understanding between the missionaries and the dancers, and it is this that Stanner was emphasizing. These questions ultimately are not only about sexual mores, though they are important, but about any surrender to the lax moral and ethical, even ritual standards of the

---

24. Lewis, *Lion*, 148.

surrounding culture. There are plenty of opportunities for us as Christians to commit fornication, in John's terms, without ever straying from the marriage bed in mind or body. John will return to this theme many times yet.

Thyatira

Thyatira is a less strategic town than those that precede it, lying in an inland valley some seventy kilometers from Pergamum. It seems that the faith community there has much to commend it—"love, faith, service, and patient endurance"—even, it seems, some improvement in its "performance indicators" (the awkward NRSV translation "your last works are greater than the first" is better rendered "your most recent efforts are greater than your beginnings"). This is not insignificant praise, for life was not likely to be easy for the Christians here, either. The town was controlled by trade guilds, which were something akin to a cross between a masonic lodge and a trade union. A resident could not work in the community unless he belonged to the guild, whose rituals again involved sacrifice and consumption of meats offered to idols. John will have no compromise. It is probable that the otherwise unidentifiable Nicolaitians, who were influential at Pergamum, and "Jezebel" at Thyatira, were taking a less rigorous, more compromised approach. My tradition of moderate Anglicanism is generally, thank God, less used to diatribes about the Great Satan, Jezebel, brutal rape and infanticide (Rev 2.20–23) directed at any with whom we disagree—even in the synods that are our primary context of debate!—but matters were more urgent in John's time, and the niceties of Anglo-Saxon debate were not a part of his discourse.

So once more we have unpleasant language and vitriol in our Scriptures. Once more we have to understand that John, like Paul, was fighting against compromise in the young and as yet unformed body of Christ. Paul suggests his opponents castrate themselves (Gal 5:12): John is more volatile still. Was there an excuse for John's vitriol? We need to remember again that this was a first century equivalent of Hitler's brown-shirts coming in the night, and John is pouring scorn on the heads of the fraternizers and compromisers. It is not pretty, but it is understandable: people were dying for their faith in Thyatira, and someone was selling them short. Despite the outburst (compare Paul's outburst in Phil 3:2), John's main God-given message to the Thyatirans is simply to endure: "hold fast to what you have until I [Christ] come" (Rev 2:25).

Babylon's Cap

Sardis

Fifty kilometers from Thyatira was Sardis, a city with a strong Jewish community, some presence of trade guilds, and a cult devoted to the goddess Cybele. It had both a proud history, having never been conquered by military force, and an infamous Achilles heel, having been twice conquered by stealth.[25] For the Christian community to effectively fall asleep with complacent nonchalance, the implication of the strong words John is commanded to write, is indictment indeed. John alludes to the memorable saying of Jesus in Matt 24:43, "if the owner of the house had known in what part of the night the thief was coming, he would have stayed awake and would not have let his house be broken into." Residents of a city twice conquered by stealth, and once destroyed by an earthquake, could not but be chilled by the comparison, if anything more apt here than in the original Palestinian setting where Jesus used the simile.

John has nothing positive to say to the people of Sardis: their complacency has reached the point of spiritual death (Rev 3:2). There are, however, a few brave individuals who have raised themselves above the sleeping morass or spiritual stupor: for them there is the promise of eternal reward. Sad to say, the harsh message to Sardis would not be out of place in much Christian culture in Western society over the past century or so: as the bumper sticker menacingly enquires, "if you were arrested for being a Christian would there be enough evidence to convict you?" Is there enough evidence to convict the Western world's Christian communities of transcendent belief, belief in a God greater than human imagining, a question that could be directed at the liberal churches? Is there enough evidence to convict us of justice-seeking compassion, be asked of the more experiential fundamentalist churches? Sardis is not a happy place to be—and ironically it appears to have slipped into its malaise with no sign of persecution or oppression.

Philadelphia

"I know that you have but little power, and yet you have kept my word" (Rev 3:8). Jürgen Moltmann has spent a lifetime teaching that Christian witness begins when we adopt the language and politics of powerlessness (see especially *The Crucified God*); it is from the lips of a crucified criminal dying on a cross, not a glorious triumphant march across the heavens, that

---

25. Harrington, *Revelation*, 68–69.

Write This Down! The Letters to the Churches (Revelation 1:1—3:22)

the victorious pronouncement "it is finished" (which I described above as "the most apocalyptic statement in salvation history") is made. In the experience of powerlessness, the Philadelphians have proved their gospel-integrity (Rev 3:8), and therefore these faithful Christ-bearers will be used to shame those who have ignored, persecuted, or abused the gospel (Rev 3:9). So faithful, indeed, have the Philadelphian believers been that they will escape the *thlipsis* (trials) that await most of the faithful (Rev 3:10).

Philadelphia was another fifty kilometers south of Sardis; like Sardis, this city had been devastated by earthquakes in the past. When the early Christian bishop Ignatius of Antioch wrote to the church there a few years after John, he was aware of strong victimization of the Christians by the politically more powerful Jewish community. The Jews had probably by John's time expelled the Christians from the synagogue (cf. John 16:2, quite different to the synoptic gospels' Mark 13:9).[26] The promise of "an open door," perhaps an echo of Paul (1 Cor 16:9, 2 Cor 2:12), is a reversal of the metaphorically slammed door of the synagogue. The spleen directed at the Jews is stringent, again: once more we must acknowledge that we are reading this in a world very different to the one in which John was writing.

Laodicea

When I was a Pentecostal Christian, and later as a charismatic in mainline church circles, it was *de rigueur* to use Rev 3:14–22 as a full-scale offensive, a weapon in a (one-way!) barrage of texts directed at those who did not appear to share my enthusiastic experience of God. Beware, those who hurl texts! I'm sure that the me of 2013 would be a victim of the verbal assaults of the me of 1979. Was my antagonism justified? It would certainly appear that the Laodicean church had "issues": were they "issues" replicated by, say, twentieth- to twenty-first-century Christians of, for example, my own Anglican denomination? Were, are, Anglicans about to be spat from the mouth of an angry God for their staid practices, drab book-prayers, and abysmal disinterest in witnessing? On the other hand, was the fact that the clergy and people of mainline churches did not parade their glossolalia like a phylactery, that they sang hymns of theological depth rather than choruses of erotic devotion to a saccharine Savior, that they tended to read more than a few selected and usually apocalyptic Scriptures about their own rapture, really a sign that not they but the Pentecostals were the Laodicean church?

26. See also Matt 10:17–18, Matt 24:9, and Luke 21:12.

There are at least two problems here. The first is that biblical texts are not missiles to be flung across barriers of hatred and suspicion. Richard Bauckham presents a second reason:

> [I]t would be a serious mistake to understand the images of Revelation as timeless symbols. Their character conforms to the contextuality of Revelation as a letter to the seven churches of Asia. Their resonances in the specific social, political, cultural and religious world of their first readers need to be understood if their meaning is to be appropriated today.[27]

To be honest, there are strengths and weaknesses in both charismatic-Pentecostal and traditional faith communities: the swing of the pendulum that initiated the charismatic enthusiasm of a Montanus or indeed of a St. Francis or a Wesley has repeated itself many times in history. Jesus warned against the parading of phylacteries, but the emphasis is on the parading, not the phylactery (Matt 23:5). Perhaps a more helpful interpretive key is another seminal Jesus saying, "You will know them by their fruits" (Matt 7:16). There are Laodicean charismatic-Pentecostal churches, and there are Laodicean traditional churches.

What had gone wrong in Laodicea? The city itself, seventy kilometers from Philadelphia, was a commercial center, wealthy, and, it seems, self-righteous. In that environment it was easy for a church, too, to become complacent, and to fail in the divine commission to stand out as what I often call (following Alan Walker) "a contrast society of Jesus."[28]

The warnings to the church at Laodicea are unambiguous, though still tinged with grace (Rev 3:19): God loves even this bland and self-satisfied church. They were written down for a particular church with particular problems of self-satisfaction and complacency. Those, however, are timeless problems. I have seen Pentecostal churches wallowing in self-importance and self-satisfaction, and I have seen traditional churches, liberal, charismatic, evangelical, and Anglo-Catholic, wallowing in the same morass. The Scriptures were written for a particular context, but they are also breathed with the Spirit of God, and in that Spirit are imbued with timelessness. To say this is not to forget their original context; we are not to believe that they lay dormant for 2,000 years with a message that Karol Wotjyla, Henry Kissinger, Julia Gillard, or John Key was the Antichrist (which is not at this point to suggest any of these figures are anti-Christian!), that a select (or

---

27. Bauckham, *Theology*, 19.
28. Walker, *Contrast*.

Write This Down! The Letters to the Churches (Revelation 1:1—3:22)

elect) few would hear that message and be raptured. Such misapplication of Scripture, though common, is demonic. The issues of the church at Laodicea have emerged in every age and culture, and the message to the first church of Laodicea is timeless for that reason.

Can Laodicea be redeemed? Yes. The anger expressed by John, despite the seeming finality of the harsh phrase "spit you out of my mouth," is redemptive anger (Rev 3:16). The Laodiceans may be "wretched, pitiable, poor, blind, and naked" (Rev 3:17), but the door of hope remains ready (Rev 3:20), and the church need only repent to enter it.

The Scriptures of our faith are multidimensional, and they can be used and misused in many ways. When I was undergoing my journey from adolescent atheism to Christianity, I wrote to a former rowing coach, whose integrity as a believer I could not but be aware of. In his reply, encouraging me to surrender to the God I was fighting, he quoted Rev 3:20 (in the RSV): "Behold, I stand at the door and knock. If any one hears my voice and opens the door, I will come in to him and eat with him, and he with me." In the months that followed I could not escape those words, and eventually returned to my mentor to surrender to his God.

The words are a powerfully evangelistic image, well captured in the famous if somewhat stilted artwork of Holman Hunt: Christ, lantern at hand, knocking on the door of your life or mine. Such use of the words removes them from their context, that of a stubborn and self-satisfied moribund church in first-century Asia Minor. But the Scriptures of our faith *are* living words, empowered by God's Spirit, empowered by the prayers and fidelity of God's people through time and space. Scriptures do not belong in a war of ideologies, as if "women, remain silent" were a card to be played, seen by an opponent, and countered with my "neither male nor female" card. But where they can speak, even out of context, to the human condition and bring the listener deeper into the mysteries of a saving God, there let them be used.

The Scriptures are not static. When I received those words from my mentor, my focus was on the "come in to him." These days, thirty years later, I might see as much energy in the latter part of the sentence, "and eat with him, and he with me." Now in those words I see something of the centrality of the eucharist—again a motif that may link the John of Revelation with the John of the Fourth Gospel and epistles, for eating is a recurring motif in the gospel-writer's narrative (John 6, especially). I doubt if it could be proved that eucharistic feeding was in John's mind as he recorded the words,[29] but if such an interpretation is consistent with the practice and

---

29. But see Harrington, *Revelation*, 30–31.

experience of God's people down through the ages, then there is an acceptable "fourth dimension" to the words. Unlike the occult interpretations that find Henry Kissinger in half a verse of Daniel or Pope John Paul II (Karol Wotjyla) in half a verse of Revelation, finding a eucharistic reference in Rev 3:20 expands and enlarges the imagery in the original words, without doing violence to their context in first-century Laodicea. In fact, both these words and the symbolism of the eucharist are primarily a "foreshadowment" of the "eschatological banquet" alluded to in many of Jesus' parables.

There are constraints to interpretation, limitations established by God's Spirit and by the self-analysis and practice of God's people through the centuries. Within those boundaries, the potentials of words such as those John wrote, so sternly, for the church at Laodicea are near infinite. In the months following the letter I received from my mentor, John's words niggled sufficiently for me to eventually commit my existence to the risen Lord. They can also speak also to us in our own faith communities as we seek to serve God in the twenty-first century: do we have an ear to listen to what the Spirit is saying to the churches (or church)?

I suspect complacency is the most powerful demon faced by contemporary Western Christians (of all flavors). The message addressed to the Laodicean church and the errors perpetrated by that church continue to hold warnings for us all. Complacent in its material wealth and in the comfort of its existence in a nonchalant society, the church was dying. There are some wonderful linguistic tricks in John's words: "poor, blind, and naked" is a heavily ironic reminder that this Laodicean church is failing to stand as a Christ-focused counterculture in a city whose wealth was based primarily on banking, eye medicine, and clothing.[30] Despite strong beginnings (Col. 2:1, 4:13–16), the Laodicean church had blended into the background and become the invisible people of God. My first parish, out beyond the Bible belt in the leafy eastern suburbs of Melbourne, was rightly proud of its building, nestling among the peppermint gums. It was architecturally designed to blend into the background of the 'burbs. Sadly it blended so well it disappeared, closed and sold years ago. A building of course is not the church, but it is a useful metaphor: surely there is an abiding warning for us all in the message to the Laodiceans?

---

30. Harrington, *Revelation*, 75.

Write This Down! The Letters to the Churches (Revelation 1:1—3:22)

CONCLUSIONS

The messages to the churches were specific messages to specific churches in a specific century. Yet they are not a closed ancient document in the way that a first-century menu or shopping list might be a closed ancient document. Bauckham, after warning that we must not look for occult messages for our own era in these chapters, adds a second warning: "if the images are not timeless symbols, but relate to the 'real' world, we need also to avoid the opposite mistake of taking them too literally as descriptive of the 'real' world and of predicted events in the 'real' world."[31] The words speak to us—and that is why, eventually, they made it into the canon of Scripture—because the issues faced by the first-century Christians of Asia Minor are timeless. Ephesus, Smyrna, Pergamum, Thyatira, Sardis, Philadelphia, and Laodicea: we have their potential. "Hear what the Spirit is saying to the Church," says *A New Zealand Prayer Book*. "Hear" indeed. Sometimes John's vision is particularly harsh: is a tendency to syncretize religions—as our European missionary forebears did when they settled on December 25 as the Feast of Nativity—really to become the harlot Jezebel? Were the continuing Jews a "synagogue of Satan"? Today I would say no. But I cannot forget the pain of my ancestors in faith, dying for their faith, from whom these words were wrung. I cannot ignore their experience any more than I can forget the pain of Paul as he wished his Galatian opponents would castrate themselves (Gal 5:12) or of the Psalmist as he wished a brutal death on the children of those who were raping and pillaging his own people (Ps 137:7).

As we conclude the messages to the seven (and how many is seven?) churches, which provide a key to understanding all of Revelation, I turn to an observation in one of the commentaries open on my desk. Wilfred Harrington, a Dominican priest to whom I have referred several times above, has this to say:

> All in all, the challenge of the Way remains. There is an incompatibility between a wholehearted following of Christ and the standards of a world unenlightened by the gospel. The danger remains that Christians can settle, too readily, for a "reasonable" approach. It is the charism of a prophet to see to the heart of things. Only the starkest words can match his uncomplicated vision. The genuine prophet will speak a message of comfort, based on the faithfulness of God, but it will never be a comfortable message. John's messages to the churches urge us to look to ourselves, to our contemporary

31. Bauckham, *Theology*, 20.

Ephesus and Philadelphia and Laodicea. The "beast" in our world is not as oppressive as the beast in John's world; it may be all the more dangerous, because more insidious.[32]

Perhaps the most powerful "beast" in Western society is the beast of sexuality. By this I do not mean the question of homosexuality that so dominates our debates, but the question of sexuality itself as a force for good and ill in the service of being human. The often empty sexuality of our society is still best captured by a remarkable twentieth-century prophet, T. S. Eliot, in four haunting lines from "The Waste Land":

> She turns and looks a moment in the glass,
> Hardly aware of her departing lover;
> Her brain allows one half-formed thought to pass:
> 'Well now that's done: and I'm glad it's over.'[33]
> ("The Waste Land," ll. 249–252)

It was no doubt ever thus, but we ask of ourselves as a Christian community, whether we propose and testify to a counterculture, a contrast society of Jesus? Do our relationships, not least our sexual mores, point to a higher standard? In Australia abortion rates, especially amongst teenage mothers, remain amongst the highest in the world. Our task is to testify to a contrast society of Jesus.

Eliot depicted scenes of lifeless sexuality as symptoms of a deeper malaise, a society that has lost decency. Do we love? Earlier in "The Waste Land," Eliot in passing makes reference to one of our John's cities:

> Unreal City
> Under the brown fog of a winter noon
> Mr. Eugenides, the Smyrna merchant,
> Unshaven, with a pocket full of currants
> C.i.f. London: documents at sight,
> Asked me in demotic French
> To luncheon at the Cannon Street Hotel
> Followed by a weekend at the Metropole.
> ("The Waste Land," ll. 207–214)[34]

It is an obscure reference, but it is a part of Eliot's extended portrayal of a modern wasteland: sexuality without love. The Cannon Street Hotel was in the midst of the commercial heart of London, while the Metropole was a

---

32. Harrington, *Revelation*, 76.
33. Eliot, *Collected Poems*, 62.
34. Ibid., 61.

Write This Down! The Letters to the Churches (Revelation 1:1—3:22)

hotel with a reputation for illicit and unwholesome sexual liaisons. Eliot is portraying a loveless sexual liaison—one of many in the poem—in the heart of a commercial city. Smyrna, London, New York, all in Eliot's hands are symbols, prosperous port cities where commercial and sexual greed unite to drown out the possibilities of God's life-giving love. In Eliot's Smyrna reference the illicit union is homosexual, but elsewhere in the poem the unions are heterosexual, and he rightly draws no distinction. Instead he draws a distinction between that which is life-giving and that which is life-denying. Eliot the prophet has seen what John the prophet saw: lives of mechanistic relations, commercial, sexual or any other form, lives in which relationships are about usage and not mutual enrichment; these are lives lived in a spiritual wasteland. John saw it, and called the Christ-bearing community to be a contrast society of Jesus, a sign of something better, a sign of a transformative and edifying love, of Paul's "more excellent way."

As suicide and self-harm remain at atrocious levels in asylum centers and Australian Indigenous communities, not least just down the road from where I write, we have hard questions to ask of ourselves and our faith communities. Do we love our neighbor in such a way as to represent a contrast society of Jesus? As lives are scarred or lost as people around us turn to drugs in the emptiness of their lives, beginning often fatal cycles of chemical dependency, dragging themselves and their families to despair, do we testify by the energy of our love to a contrast society of Jesus? Our sisters and brothers in the first century faced many opportunities to succeed or fail as such a society, and so do we. Despite their failures, even those of the Laodiceans and the Sardisians (but were the intolerant Ephesians or the over-tolerant Thyatirans and those at Pergamum any better?), the gospel steadily took root in these communities and they went on to testify to the faith of and in Christ. John saw the implications of a Christian community that lost its ability to stand firm: Babylon then conquers, or, as Eliot put it, we become "Dead mountain mouth of carious teeth that cannot spit" ("The Wasteland," l. 339).[35] John wrote to the seven churches to wake them from their stupor.

Ultimately Christ overcomes even their failures and ours: we need to live as though we believe it. To that end, having delivered his message to the seven churches, John turns to deliver his message of God's coming final triumph over evil and death in all its forms.

---

35. Ibid., 66.

3

Riders of the Apocalypse and Other Lurid Scenes (Revelation 4:1–9:21)

THAT WE ARE MOVING into the realm of the visionary is clear as soon as John moves from the specific letters, targeted to the churches, to the general vision related to what we must now call "the church," all his audiences (us unexpectedly included). In the book of Revelation the heavenly voice, first heard at 1:8, is the voice of divine authority. But John's language is no longer describing anything resembling our day-to-day experience: emeralds, for example, do not generally look like rainbows (a detail leading one commentator to remark "a statement which teases the imagination out of all thought"[1]). The synesthesia mentioned previously is expressed not only in the reconnection of senses, but also in the unexpected rearrangement of visual images. When John speaks of a door, a trumpet-like voice (Rev 4:1a), travel to a different place (Rev 4:1b), a figure appearing "as if" jasper and carnelian (Rev 4:3a), or describes an aura around a throne as "an emerald that looks like a rainbow" (Rev 4:3b), he is warning us that his vision is taking us into an unfamiliar realm.

It is not unfair to say my Nimbin[2] friends were doing something similar when they attempted to describe the experiences encountered during periods of chemical enhancement. The rock poets did the same, most memorably Lennon and McCartney with their blatant allusions to the drug LSD in "Lucy in the Sky with Diamonds," or Bob Dylan's surreal but

---

1. G. B. Caird, quoted by Leon Morris, in Morris, *Revelation*, 86.

2. Nimbin, a small town in Northern New South Wales, is often considered the "hippie" or "alternative lifestyle" capital of Australia.

Riders of the Apocalypse and Other Lurid Scenes (Revelation 4:1–9:21)

powerfully poetic lyrics of "Mr. Tambourine Man".[3] They utilized conventions and imagery shared by at least most within what was at the time a subversive subculture. But without being critical of the rock poets, of whom I am an admirer, their highly individualized and interiorized culture, while throwing a few gauntlets at the feet of post-war society's leadership, and ousting a few McCarthies, did not in the end offer a potently constructive counterculture. The darkly symbolic moment when Ohio National Guardsmen brutally killed four students at Kent State University in 1970, an obscene act of state-sanctioned overkill seen by many to represent the end of the hippie idyll, was ultimately not a definitive moment. The Summer of Love faded into dysfunctionality, and the hippie revolution failed primarily because, once the state troopers had gone home, once the love-ins were over, there was no edifying counterculture to establish. Wearing flowers in my hair[4] and practicing free sex cannot liberate society for long, and the true believers were still entrapped in the morass of human sin in all its complexity. Free sex and chemical dependencies soon became new forms of oppression, and the practitioners of these new creeds were subject to a whole new set of social and spiritual demons from which some have never escaped. However, synesthesia would not disappear, lyrically or experientially: Dolores O'Riordan would, for example, sing of a "psychedelic breeze."[5]

John was at one level not dissimilar to the more surreal rock poets (or their forebears, most notably William Blake and S. T. Coleridge). He was using conventions, linguistic signs and symbols which were more accessible to his original audience than they are to us. In Jewish literature there is no precedent for entering the holiest places of heaven, and Jewish writers of the time soon took umbrage at the high claims made particularly by the authors of the Fourth Gospel ("we beheld his glory," John 1:14; at Acts 7:54 the same claim leads to martyrdom) and Revelation ("Come up here and I will show you . . ." Rev 4:1). There are, however, parallels to John's imagery of a glimpsed heavenly door. In a document written at a similar

---

3. Lyrics may be found at http://www.bobdylan.com/us/songs/mr-tambourine-man or, in hard copy, in Dylan, *Lyrics*, 153.

4. Scott McKenzie sang a song "Be Sure to Wear Flowers in Your Hair", penned by The Mamas and the Poppas' John Philips. It was an iconic hippie anthem not least because it was written primarily to unofficially advertise the Monterey Folk Festival, in 1967. It gained anthem status also in the ill-fated Czechoslovakian "Prague Spring" uprising.

5. From the 1999 Cranberries song "Sorry Son," on non-US editions of the album *Bury the Hatchet*.

time to Revelation, the visionary author records a moment "when Isaiah spoke with Hezekiah the words of righteousness and faith" and "they all heard a door being opened and the voice of the Spirit."[6] This is not to suggest that the author of this early Christian document borrowed from our author or *vice versa*, but to recognize that John drew on a pool of images that readily communicated ideas in his era that may be more inaccessible and weird to us today. "Flowers in my hair" will be a strange image perhaps even to today's children—indicating perhaps only a preference for organic jewelry-substitution—but to a California or Nimbin hippie in 1969 the phrase represented a whole idealized lifestyle of freedom from all sexual, moral, legal, and fiscal constraints (it was, however, always going to end in tears, Christian doctrine would suggest, this side of the *eschaton*). Linguistic conventions are not so much a code as a shared set of images that convey a community's highest values. US President Obama intuitively sensed that in Darwin when he chanted "Aussie! Aussie! Aussie!" There was only ever going to be one response, as he masterfully entered into his audience's narrative.

Linguistic conventions do not always belong to subcultures, like the hippies of the mid-twentieth century or the Christians of late first-century Asia Minor. We are constantly borrowing terminology from small subsections of our shared lives and applying it to some other part of our shared lives. We would be using linguistic conventions if we spoke of the blowing of a whistle (though the term is confused when we speak of "whistle-blowers," who blow an entirely different kind of whistle: context is everything!). As a person involved in sports for decades I understand that a whistle signifies either a temporary or a permanent cessation of play, and as a writer I will assume that this metaphor is accessible to all but the most sport-unaware of my intended audience. (The term whistle-blower is probably more archaic, referring to the old policeman's whistle drawing attention to a crime.) This type of borrowing and adapting of terms is technically called "metonymy": the shared experience of whistles blowing means that we know that a whistle means so much more than just a small, tuneless but piercing wind instrument. We know it means an interruption or conclusion of proceedings: we did *not*, however, know that until someone, some time, decided it was a good way to breathe order into the chaos of sports events. We would not know it if we were living in a remote community, utterly unexposed

---

6. "Martyrdom and Ascension of Isaiah" 6:6, translated by M. A. Knibb, in Charlesworth, *Apocalyptic*, 164.

Riders of the Apocalypse and Other Lurid Scenes (Revelation 4:1–9:21)

to the mores and codes or sporting societies, like a remote Amazonian or Australian tribal culture. It is an agreed convention.

Language in any era works as a vast resource pool, within agreed conventions. As soon as John wrote of a heavenly door, his audience knew we were moving into a highly privileged experience of an encounter with God. It is a warning, the first reminder after the "letters to the churches," that this vision given to John is transcendent and other-worldly, heavenly and authoritative. The heavenly door is used by John to alert his audience to some conventions that are to follow. He is not using a secret code, whose matrices are known only to a select in-crowd wielding power over hapless believers, as some conspiracy theorists suggest of the early church. He is using signs and symbols, conventions available to anyone who wishes to encounter the risen Christ whose message he is transcribing. Certainly references to heavenly doors, voices, and obscure celestial jewels (the words here rendered "jasper and carnelian" were generalized terms whose meaning we cannot be certain of today) would have been reasonably obscure to those in the corridors of Roman power. But conspiracy theorists reading Revelation miss this fundamental point: John was writing as an underdog for underdogs. If a little "in-house" terminology could keep the enemy at bay, all well and good: that was a bonus. As we enter his vision, noting the door he has entered, we are entering a realm of open secrets, conveyed by means of symbols and images shared by author and audience, accessible to anyone sympathetically interested enough to enquire as to their meaning.

Language and its words and symbols can invite or repel. Many years ago I stayed for a fortnight with a group of broadcasting cadets in a private hotel in Wellington, New Zealand. As cadets—young, would-be wild men and women in our late teens and early twenties, setting out to take the world by storm—we had our own shared codes. We shared, for example, dress codes, much as in New Zealand today (though not in Darwin where I now live, probably for climactic reasons) a conspicuous subculture of young males wear their shorts with their waste line perilously close to the bottom of their buttocks, boxers conspicuous. Originally a prison look (because belts were confiscated to prevent suicide or assault), this form of clothing is itself a language, a symbolic structure that serves to repel those like me who do not like it, maintaining the boundaries of an in-group and keeping the masses beyond. Language can serve a similar purpose, and back in our hotel we were ensuring that our language—including broadcasting terminology and "youth-speak"—as well as the experiences we shared each day set us apart from the other diners. We were, however, subverted by another group. For also staying in the hotel was a group of Middle Eastern men, who increasingly destabilized our raucous conviviality by watching and pointing at us and then laughing loudly. They spoke in their own language, unsettling us. Within that language their symbolic narrative was unavailable to us, rendering us "other," "outside." Luke may be hinting at a similar experience, albeit seen from the believers' "in" perspective, in Acts 17:18–19: "some Epicurean and Stoic philosophers debated with him. Some said, 'What does this babbler want to say?' Others said, 'He seems to be a proclaimer of foreign divinities.' (This was because he was telling the good news about Jesus and the resurrection.)" The onlookers could not grasp, even with a common language, the symbolic structure of the Christians' (in this case Paul's) discourse.

My Wellington experience was at the time profoundly unsettling, but the memory offers a reminder why conquering cultures will often set about systematically destroying the languages and with them the symbolic systems of the peoples they conquer. The Romans, probably willfully, destroyed, for example, the Etruscan language, the Hapsburgs sought to destroy the Czech language in Moravia, the British sought to eradicate Māori, and successfully obliterated, for example, all Tasmanian Aboriginal languages.[7] The linguistic cost of colonialism has been immeasurable: the majority of mainland Indigenous Australian languages have been annihilated to the point that linguistics scholar John Lynch observes "Most of the languages spoken [in Australia] two hundred years ago will not survive the next fifty years."[8] Lynch records a catena of lost languages in the Polynesian and Melanesian contexts alone, and, while some loss has been a sort of collateral damage of Colonial expansionism, some loss was a result of calculated programs of "linguisticide". It was a brave stand by our missionary forebears in regions such as Arnhem Land or Aotearoa/New Zealand to recognize the sacred value of Indigenous languages and to do their best to preserve them. Usually, but not always, the symbolic structures embedded in the languages were also lost.

Back in my hotel dining room, we Europeans were the dominant culture, but the Middle Eastern men slowly undermined our confidence: we were glad when they left. The Czech peasants ultimately overcame the Hapsburgs' linguisticide, and at least some Polynesian, Melanesian, and

7. Lynch, *Pacific Languages*, 68–69.
8. Ibid., 269.

Riders of the Apocalypse and Other Lurid Scenes (Revelation 4:1–9:21)

Australian Indigenous languages are fighting back. The Romans would have been uneasy at the peculiar terminology and phraseology that was being used by Christian (and Jewish) writers such as our John. But, despite the misreadings made by some critics who are determined to damn Christians with their conspiracy theories, the Christians were not the dominant culture. Like the Arabic-speaking men in the dining room, they were a subversive minority culture, holding tenaciously to their symbols. In fact, Christians ultimately came to the attention of their communities by the subversive quality of their love (1 Cor 13 again), compassion, and moral propriety, not from the point of a sword. They, it should be noted, were sharing common languages with the dominant cultures around them, but their symbolic structures were sometimes vastly different, and slowly they prevailed in a context of oppression.

The door that John enters provides an honored glimpse beyond normal human sight: the jewels, whether semi-precious or precious, that describe "the one seated there" are a reminder that when "the things of heaven" are at stake they are beyond the power of human telling. John uses obscure imagery because he is in any case reluctant to describe God, to limit God to the normal language of human beings, the language used for everyday things. The untranslatable "jasper and carnelian," or the rainbow-like aura around the celestial throne are conventions warning the audience that we are here entering the indescribable. Too many sacred mushrooms, or a dose of hippie hooch? Not so: John will soon anchor his language in the great poetry of the Jewish tradition, poetry that his audiences immediately recognized as the poetry of divine encounter. The image of thrones surrounding the primary celestial throne immediately reminded his audience of a similar vision of Micaiah related in 1 Kgs (1 Kgs 22:19): "I saw the Lord sitting on his throne, with all the host of heaven standing beside him to the right and to the left of him." John is claiming Hebrew Scriptural precedents for his own vision: the number twenty-four, while not having the innumerable antecedents of the number seven, is a figure repeated enough times in the Old Testament to suggest "a divinely ordained number" (most noticeably in 1 Chr 23—27). By making generalized allusions to Old Testament imagery, John is conveying the solemn nature of the vision he is recounting and providing "imprimatur" to his writing.

Perhaps even more self-conscious is John's echo of Ezek 1 (especially Ezek 1:26): although the gathered beings around the celestial throne differ in number and appearance, the imagery is a clear enough echo of Ezekiel's imagery to suggest that thematic links are being established. Well-versed in Hebrew Scriptures (for as yet, remember, the early Christians did not have the New Testament), John's audiences would have made connections: was not Ezekiel a prophet in exile (Ezek 1:1, cf. Rev 1:9)? Did not Ezekiel stand up, face up to the tyrannies of oppressive totalitarian states (Ezek 25:1—32:32) and foretell the establishment of God's glorious kingdom (Ezek 43:2: "there, the glory of the God of Israel was coming from the east; the sound was like the sound of mighty waters; and the earth shone with his glory")? John, however, is not slavishly emulating or repeating Ezekiel's symbolism: for Ezekiel, Babylon, and the Hebrews' exile there, is a part of the stern punitive action of God (Ezek 17:11–21). Babylon will receive shorter shrift in the book of Revelation, but John's case remains the same as Ezekiel's: "God's will be done on earth," and the nations and their leaders are but tools in the hands of the Creator.

John is also referring to the heavenly hymnody of Isaiah 6 (Rev 4:8). Allusions to the great hymns of praise of Jewish liturgy and Scripture were a major part of both Jewish and early Christian liturgy, and they were therefore extremely familiar to John's audience, giving them a sense of solidarity as they faced the overwhelming disinterest or hostility of the surrounding Roman culture. They remain a part of Christian liturgy and hymnody today, but there is an increasing risk, as churches strive for a "relevant" worship image to enhance their mission and evangelistic profile, that these great resource pools of meaning are being lost. In the ancient faith communities they served a theological purpose beyond expression of praise to God: they reminded the gathered faithful that as they prayed to and praised the unseen God, they did so not on their own but surrounded by the residents of eternity, the faithful who had gone before them and the angels of heaven. So profound are the hymns of praise sung before the throne of God, John tells us, that the very hierarchy (as it were) of heaven falls prostrate before the divine throne. It is no accident that the *Sanctus*, "Holy, holy, holy is the Lord God of hosts", is a key moment in formal liturgy two thousand years later. Personally, when I intone those words, spoken or sung at the sacred eucharist, I bow (albeit only slightly, for fear of pretentiousness!) to remember in awe that these are timeless words, and that as we gather at God's Table we do so not alone but surrounded by the invisible hosts of heaven.

In the twenty-first century these sentiments can seem twee. Yet I take them seriously precisely because our forebears in faith took them seriously. When John and his people gathered in thanksgiving (which is what

Riders of the Apocalypse and Other Lurid Scenes (Revelation 4:1–9:21)

"eucharist" means, even though it was still only evolving into the shape it has now), they took strength from the knowledge of the presence of the heavenly host around them. Citing Isa 6, for example, they knew, as the Roman equivalents of Hitler's Brown-shirts came to smash their properties and take away their loved ones, that Rome and its Caesar did not have the final word: "you [Lord] created all things, and by your will they existed and were created" (Rev 4:11).

As alluded to in passing, above, John in Revelation 4 picks up, momentarily, an emphasis on God as Creator. He will return to this again in Revelation 10 and Rev 14:7, before he turns to the crescendo of New Creation at Rev 21:1–5. It is an underlying assumption of both Old and New Testament Scriptures, and a radical one. To us, well formed in the assumptions of creation theology (by which I do not mean the seven-day creation emphasis of fundamentalism), the notion of a single source of creation is potentially passé. Luke Timothy Johnson celebrates the centrality of this theme in his study of the Nicene Creed: "This understanding of creation not simply as an event in the distant past but above all as a constant and present activity of God is the dominant testimony of Scripture."[9] Even in a post-modern culture in which the notion of a divine Creator is scorned, the scorn is nevertheless directed primarily at the Judeo-Christian (and Islamic) notion of a single creating entity. It is, to the outspoken "evangelical" atheists of the twenty-first century, the Judeo-Christian or perhaps "Abramic" (by which word Islam is included) Creator that does not exist. No energy is spent on bus advertising or at university seminars or at the Global Atheist Convention demonstrating that, for example, the Polynesian mythologies of creation, or the ancient coming-into-being narratives of the Dreamtime, or the Sumerian, Egyptian, Greek, Roman or Etruscan narratives of creation are false.

This twenty-first century anti-Creator mindset is the shadow cast by the deep belief held by Jews, Christians and Muslims: where there is deep belief there will be antagonism to deep belief. The Jewish people began to stand out from their neighbors as they developed their belief in a single creator God. Christians and Jews of the first century appeared odd to their Roman neighbors for this belief; the Romans called this monotheistic tenacity "atheism," because the Jews and Christians denied the gods of Rome. John does not often turn openly to revisit this seminal belief, but it undergirds all his theology:

9. Johnson, *Creed*, 95.

> You are worthy, our Lord and God,
> to receive glory and honor and power,
> for you created all things,
> and by your will they existed and were created (Rev 4:11).

The theme of confidence in the Creator's control, sneeringly dismissed by today's antitheists, was no less sneeringly dismissed by the Roman overlords that surrounded John's audiences. The Christians dug deep into their experience—in worship, in fellowship, and in study of the Hebrew Scriptures—and found confidence: the "plan of the mystery hidden for ages in God who created all things" (Eph 3:9), or the experience of the one who is "before all things, and in him all things hold together" (Col 1:17) uplifted them in times of trial.

In Revelation 4, the hymns of praise could be spoken by a Christian or a Jew: "There is nothing in chapter 4 which could not have been written by a non-Christian Jewish visionary."[10] By chapter 5 this is no longer true; remarkably, the acts of creation and redemption, and offerings of worship, are being attributed not only to the one God of Hebrew worship, but to the crucified Jew who had died at Roman hands only a few decades earlier.

For in chapter 5 the author introduces the pivotal figure that on some thirty occasions he calls "the Lamb." It is strange terminology, though perhaps no less so than the other significant terms of the chapter. Here we have once more the throne, a scroll with seven seals, and harps and golden bowls and incense. We have myriads of adoring creatures, the 24 elders once more, bitter tears, and overt Hebrew scriptural allusions—the Lion of Judah, the Root of David. The language of apocalyptic is heating up, and for the first time John makes a radical step away from the apocalyptic language of Judaism. For now, with moves unlikely to gain the favor of his Jewish neighbors any more than he has previously sought to gain favor with his Roman neighbors, he associates the striking figure that he has called the Lamb with "the Lion of the tribe of Judah" and "the Root [descendant] of David" (Rev 5:5). The referencing of a savior figure as a "Lion" is to Gen 49:9, where "Judah is a lion's whelp" (see also Deut 33:22). The "Root of David" (see also Rev 22:16), clearly a term designed to drive to the heart of Jewish self-understanding, echoes Isa 11:1–10, in which a messianic figure will appear to re-establish the line and authority of the seminal Hebrew King David. Again: John is applying these high expectations to the crucified criminal Jesus within three to six decades after the events of Jesus' life

---

10. Bauckham, *Theology*, 38.

Riders of the Apocalypse and Other Lurid Scenes (Revelation 4:1–9:21)

and death. In order not to be considered absolutely insane, these majestic and celestial claims for a recent living figure must resonate with his audience's sense of the awesome presence of the risen Christ in experiences of worship, fellowship, and scriptural study. Anything less than that (for example, if we claimed that Elvis Presley or Che Guevara is alive and well) would be unlikely to inspire believers to risk their lives for their faith.

The liturgical language of chapter 5 is once again a reminder that in liturgy, believers stand not merely in the presence of those bonded by a common aim, like a passionate football crowd or a political party, but in the presence of unseen hosts, "myriads of myriads and thousands of thousands" (Rev 5:11). But now John takes the daring leap that was first foreshadowed in Rev 1:13, when he "turned and saw one like the Son of Man." Now he overtly associates Jesus of Nazareth with the Creator God, God who at Rev 4:11 was pronounced "worthy . . . to receive glory and honor and power." In a breathtakingly audacious leap, that same "power and wealth and wisdom and might and honor and glory and blessing" is—twice—ascribed to the Lamb, immediately identified as "one who was slaughtered" (Rev 5:12–13). By Rev 7:17 the Lamb's place at the throne will be even less ambiguous than it is here, where he still remains between the throne and the elders: by Rev 7:17 the Lamb is at the center of the throne. Yet even in the earlier scene, where the Lamb's physical location *near* the throne suggests a hint of hierarchical subordination, the hymns addressed to him are unambiguously divine. It would be a brave baseball or cricket tragic or political aficionado that ascribed Creator-status to a figure who died only a few decades before: even Joe DiMaggio or Don Bradman are unlikely to achieve such accolades, while John F. Kennedy and Robert Menzies remain firmly earth-bound fifty years after their deaths. It would be a still more manic political or sporting devotee who indicated that he or she had witnessed the hosts of heaven singing in adulation of their hero (see Rev 5:14).

Why does John weep (Rev 5:4)? Later we will find the earth's mighty (who Luke sees "brought down . . . from their thrones"—Luke 1:52) weeping because Babylon has fallen (Rev 18:9–13). But John is weeping not for selfish loss, but for another reason: the delay of the end (Rev 5:4, 6:10). To John this seems to be a bitter delay in the process of initiating God's reign of justice. But while John weeps that there is as yet no end to human suffering, he is privileged to see the glorious future ending that is in the hands of God. The vision of the Lamb unrolling the scroll is a glimpse into an as yet unrealized future, and it is John's task to transcribe his futuristic glimpse in order to comfort his people who are entrapped in the suffering present. He goes on to narrate his highly graphic vision of the four apocalyptic horsemen. The message they carry is unlikely to be of great comfort to those *outside* the community of faith, for they ride out carrying conquest (that is to say, conquest of those who are not the faithful), slaughter, subjugation (the scales of Rev 6:6), and death. These are what might be termed the "shadow side" of the horsemen's task. It is not John's task to bring comfort to those who are not his audience!

For the faithful there is an alternative perspective. As the first rider, astride his white horse, comes out to conquer, it is to conquer the enemies of God and God's faithful people (Rev 6:2). When the second rider comes out on his red horse, he removes the veneers of decency and coexistence from society, leaving those who are not God's people to slaughter one another (Rev 6:4). Some of us have read William Golding's *Lord of the Flies*; most of us have read or witnessed reports of the carnages of contemporary wars, or the brute bestiality of US troops and officials in Guantanamo Bay or Abu Ghraib, or of British attacks on civilians in Helmand Province, Afghanistan. In his first-century context, John is bravely claiming that the rider will destroy the much-vaunted *Pax Romana*, by which the Caesar claimed to provide protection for his subjects in return for their taxes and obeisance.[11]

As John narrates the vision there is no guarantee that the faithful are preserved from the wholesale slaughter. Rev 6:9 reminds us that suffering has ever been the lot of those who follow Christ, and Rev 6:11 indicates that there will be yet more called to die for their faith. There have been countless more in the centuries since John wrote. But there is a contrast. For those outside the community of the faithful, all slaughter, John suggests, is suffering without hope. "Abandon hope, all ye who enter here," sees Dante above the gates of hell. The Christians who suffer and die do so in the hope of resurrection. They do so even if they, like John, cry out "how long?" (Rev 6:10) as they await the *eschaton*.

The third apocalyptic rider releases a peculiar blight across the face of the earth. The metaphor John uses is elusive, but the scales are the scales of commerce, by which a portion of the earth's populace is locked in greed while a portion is locked in abject poverty. We might wonder at the 1 percent of the richest US citizens who are desperately seeking to ensure that no political move ever succeeds in imposing fair taxes on them, and query

---

11. Boring, *Revelation*, 122.

Riders of the Apocalypse and Other Lurid Scenes (Revelation 4:1–9:21)

why the CEOs of US firms earn 475 times the amount earned by average workers. This amount can be disputed to some extent: the ACTU's Executive PayWatch 2010 report, available online,[12] cites an Australian figure of 1:100, whilst *The Wall Street Journal*'s marketwatch.com cites one example of a US executive, Fred Hassan, who as CEO of Schering Plough, received remuneration "more than 1,100 times higher" than the national average wage—and oversaw the sacking of 16,000 workers.[13] The comparison of Caesar's wealth with that of the average member of a church community in first-century Asia Minor would be illuminating.

We might remember too that there are third-world or "global south" communities beneath the bridges of US turnpikes, that there are families living atop the garbage dumps of Manila, and that Australian Indigenous communities are trapped in cycles of low life expectancy, chemical dependence, fiscal mismanagement, and domestic violence. In Rev 18:11–12 we will find an equally if not more disturbing image of economic apocalypse, as Babylon's merchants who have plied their trade in opulence find their markets gone and have no place to flee God's wrath.

The fourth horseman rides a sickly colored horse and releases disease across the earth. This too is a ageless image: in John's time a blight the likes of bubonic plague could decimate a population in weeks, while diseases that we consider largely under control today—typhoid, diphtheria, malaria, or tuberculosis for starters—were only a whisker away from the population at any given time. As I grew up in the 1970s, the educational film strips (as they then were) were smug in their assurance that disease was soon to be a thing of the past (along with the need to work more than a few hours each week!), and humankind was on the cusp, almost, of self-inflicted immortality. In the decades since we have not only seen how vulnerable immeasurable numbers of the world's population are to previously unknown viruses such as HIV/AIDS, but also the rise of staphylococci in our hospitals. We have witnessed the vulnerability of our artificially nurtured food supplies to genetic failure (bovine encephalitis or "mad cow disease" being the most obvious), and we have watched with hearts momentarily in mouths as viruses such as H1N1 have jumped species to provide international apoplexy and pandemic fears (though humankind, as T. S. Eliot once said, "cannot bear too much reality,"[14] and lapses quickly back into indifference). Here,

---

12. ACTU, "Executive Paywatch 2010," Paragraph 4.
13. Coombes, "Personal Finance."
14. "Go, go, go, said the bird: human kind / Cannot bear very much reality." From

too, John does not offer quarantined protection to the faith community, but continues to build a contrast between those who die without hope and the white-robed ranks who die in the embrace of Christ.

After the four horsemen make their way across the earth, two further seals of the scroll are opened, and their contents are let loose across history. The fifth seal does not release an apocalyptic rider, but allows John to see the saints of history as they await the consummation of history and time. The expectant longing of the saints is contrasted with those without divine hope, for whom the closure of life and time is not a source of hope and inspiration. As it happens, the saints echo John's earlier tears of longing, but there is no bitterness in their tears. The saints' sentiment is captured in Samuel Stone's famous hymn "The Church's One Foundation"; in Stone's depiction, the faithful gather in the knowledge that sin and degradation continues unabated around them, and they long for the final reign of God:

> Though with a scornful wonder
> the world sees her oppressed,
> by schisms rent asunder,
> by heresies distressed,
> yet saints their watch are keeping,
> their cry goes up, "How long?"
> and soon the night of weeping
> shall be the morn of song.

I remember singing that hymn in a tiny but packed church, All Saints', Dunedoo, near Dubbo in New South Wales. A large number of us had gathered for an historic induction, late in January, with temperatures well into the mid-forties °C. As we sang the line "their cry goes up, 'How long?,'" wilting eyes met across the nave, particularly those of the clergy, duly robed for the occasion: I doubt the line has ever been sung with such feeling as it was that sunbaked evening. I am not intending to trivialize: trifling though they may seem by contrast with the great themes of faith, these moments remind us of connections between text and experience, and our small experiences can illuminate the great themes of faith.

A sixth seal was one whose loosed energy should strike awe in the hearts of those who know the unparalleled power of unleashed tectonic energy. While I would hate to get into a fatuous argument of "my earthquake is bigger than your cyclone," there is no doubt that the sudden bewildering energy of tectonic pressure, released without warning, is a thing of horror.

"Burnt Norton," Eliot, *Collected Poems*, 178.

Riders of the Apocalypse and Other Lurid Scenes (Revelation 4:1–9:21)

In New Zealand when, in 2010 and 2011, devastating earthquakes shattered lives, infrastructure and buildings, there was no warning. Christchurch, principal city of New Zealand's South Island, was not, at least in uninformed thought, even considered to be at risk from major earthquake. Growing up around the splintered fault lines around Wellington, the capital of New Zealand at the foot of the North Island and considered the most likely population center to be facing the destruction unleashed by earthquake, I know only too well the deep, almost subsonic rumble that precedes a "big one," and the bewildering "balancelessness" that undermines all self-confidence as the normally safe earth shifts beneath you. As a New Zealander I know the inescapability and brute serendipity of earthquake, yet even so I cannot pretend to imagine the ghastly horror of Christchurch's two big ones, or the countless aftershocks that have been a part of the lives of residents of Christchurch and surrounds ever since. In my childhood boarding school, well known for its inflexible brick vulnerability to earthquake, I used to feel tremors at night and long for the moment when they were over: we were trained to scurry beneath desks or beds if they became too strong, although the aftermath of Christchurch tells us, had a big one come, the protection afforded would have been minimal.

"When he opened the sixth seal, I looked, and there came a great earthquake" (Rev 6:12), but the vision given to John does not end there. The sun is darkened (even a solar eclipse is an eerie, if harmless experience), the moon turns blood-red (how well I recall the seemingly ash-stained moon in the days after the Australian Ash Wednesday bushfires in 1983, and following the 2013 fires in southern Australia, New Zealanders have again experienced spectacular dust- and ash-filled sunsets), "and the stars of the sky fell to the earth." Earthquake, darkened sun, reddened moon: these are eerie but occasional human experiences. As Judith Durham conveyed when she sang "when the stars began to fall"[15] with The Seekers, that last image shifts from the occasional to the surreal (and, we would add, physically impossible). But the vision John is conveying was never intended to be scientific analysis: this is the stuff of cosmic terror. This is the stuff of all the terror we can imagine (and since 9/11 and Kuta Beach, the latter the location of the 2002 Bali bombings, our Western imaginations have been enlarged once more) and then some. If "shock and awe" is a military term describing maximized initial onslaught, John the Seer is depicting

---

15. From the traditional song "When the Stars Begin to Fall." Durham was lead singer of the 1960s Australian folk group The Seekers.

something far greater. The images of the earth's powerful people hiding in the paralysis of fear (Rev 6:15) is both apocalyptic and realistic; media images and descriptions of the final moments of Saddam Hussein and Muanmar Gadhafi remind us, however obscenely, that tyrants too, if not tyrants especially, fear death.

Chapter 6 ends with a rhetorical question: "who is able to stand?" It is an echo of Nah 1:6 and Mal 3:2. The expected answer, within the Christian community, is "no one, but for the grace of God." That there is hope of standing, however, is partially revealed in the very next sentence (remember chapters and verses were added centuries later), when the verb "to stand" is predicated of the angels (Rev 7:1); it will soon be predicated of all who stay faithful to God, human or otherwise.[16] The emphasis is on fidelity to God. A primary part of fidelity to God will always be worship, and the vision of John moves on to a scene of worship, as 144,000 bearing the divine seal, plus an unnumbered multitude of those clothed in robes paradoxically whitened in the blood of the Lamb (Rev 7: 9–12), gather together in praise. 144,000? This strange number had been much abused, notoriously in the popular teaching of Jehovah's Witnesses. It is outlined with tribal detail in Rev 7:5–8 and means little more than "the perfect number," "a vast throng beyond all reckoning."[17] The twelve tribes are not a genealogical description, but a sign of the inclusion and perfection of the number of the people of God—John's twelve tribes do not correspond with any Hebrew scriptural listing of tribes. Revelation 7:5–8 says no more nor less than Rev 7:9, and while the 144,000 are "sealed" and the "vast multitude" of martyrs merely robed, there is no ranking to differentiate, because the scene is not about those gathered, but about the One in the center: "John lets us see the suffering love of the One who dies for others enthroned and ruling at the heart of the universe."[18]

Praise and worship, in which the countless throng gather, is in itself the countercultural activity *par excellence* that will set the people of God aside—a detail that sits in strong opposition to the oft-presented argument "I don't have to go to church to be a Christian." The countless crowd, those who have survived "the great trial" (Rev 7:14), stand unified, singing sacred praise to God and, in the same breath, praise to the conquering Lamb. This union of God and Lamb is another remarkable liturgical and theological

---

16. Rev 7:9, 11:4, 14:1, and above all Rev 15:2.
17. Boring, *Revelation*, 131.
18. Ibid., 132.

amalgamation of the Jesus-figure and the incomparable God, one which would be unfathomable and indeed blasphemous only decades before. As noted previously, John, like many of the New Testament writers, is striving towards trinitarian language.

The crowd of those worshiping in unity, together praising God and the Lamb, is contrasted with another unspecific mass of humanity, loosely referred to in John's vision as "peoples and multitudes and nations and languages" (Rev 17:15) or "those who live on earth . . . every nation and tribe and language and people" (Rev 14:6). Generally this kind of contrast in the Scriptures has given rise to a dominant Christian doctrine referred to by scholars as an "exclusivist" doctrine of salvation (or "soteriology," from the Greek word *sotēr*, for "savior"). We need once more to be careful here as we interpret: Christianity has generally held to various doctrines of "salvation in Christ alone" (based not least on Acts 4:12) or *extra ecclesiam nulla salus* ("outside the church there is no salvation"). This doctrine is often used, particularly in tandem with apocalyptic writings such as the book of Revelation, to instill the fear of God into listeners, frightening them into faith. It also has the effect of inculcating great grief in the hearts of those whose children, siblings, parents and other loved ones do not ostensibly share their faith. In a series of studies designed to emphasize the emotional cost of missionary service, former CMS missionary and erstwhile Archbishop of Melbourne David Penman spoke of the grief of being on missionary service in Pakistan when his father died, and of being "unable to know which side of the kingdom he was on." It was a memory designed to convince his listeners of the merit of missionary service, placing it perhaps in the light of Matt 8:22. Of his credible commitment, self-sacrifice, and the sacrifice of his family, and of the same of all sincere missionaries, I had nor have no doubt. But it is an example of a harsh "line in the sand" doctrine of salvation: does it find authority in a piece of writing like the book of Revelation? Are children and grandchildren lost to us for all eternity when they refuse the faith we value? If they are, then surely it would be the realms of heaven, at least as much as the pits of hell, that echoed to the sound of inconsolable wailing, even if the tears are to be wiped away by the Lamb himself (Rev 7:17)?

While this is a fundamental question posed by reading the book of Revelation, I'm not sure it can be answered here.[19] It is in fact not a question John or any other apocalyptic writer was setting out to answer. John was dealing with the harsh realities of persecution, perseverance, and apostasy.

---

19. Wilfred Harrington has provided an outstanding assessment of the issues in an excursus to his commentary. Harrington, *Revelation*, 230–32.

Babylon's Cap

In such a context it was not helpful to blur the boundaries of belonging: when the Roman soldiers were using clubs and the threat of becoming lion-tucker, it was not wise to offer easy options, to suggest that if you compromise grace will still reach you, God will still redeem you, love will still breathe eternity into you. But the boundaries *are* blurred: God is not forced to make people recipients of revelation (and therefore salvation) because of church membership. Perhaps for now a hint from Karl Barth, who I consider to be the greatest theologian of the last century, must suffice:

> [A]t the given place in the Old Testament as well as the New Testament we always find men who appear not to be recipients of revelation at all. And God is not bound to this membership; in the Old Testament, at all events, figures are constantly turning up, who, quite away from the given place, outside the nation Israel, seem nevertheless to be recipients of God's revelation.[20]

To be, in Barth's terms, "recipients of God's revelation" is the same as being "recipients of God's salvation." There are many who are simply not bothered by the deeper questions of salvation. The evangelistic approach to such people used to be the formulaic "if you died tonight where would you go?" approach. Today that is likely to be met with a snort of derision: "Who cares?" or "Into the nitrogen cycle." I am not convinced that this approach to evangelism is Christlike: despite the judgment-weight of some of his parables (see especially Luke 12:20), Jesus himself never browbeats those who approach him into faith-submission. The "disinterested" may well be disinterested simply because we, as Christ-bearers, have done so little to make faith (or eternity) interesting. And there are others, too: what of those many individuals who have left the church (in all its forms) as a result of horrendous experiences such as sexual abuse, and whose decision to leave is therefore clearly not defective? Are they outside John's vision of the saved? These are questions we shall return to as we approach the crescendo of John's vision.

For now, though, we are left with one of John's great poetic passages, as the multitude from every nation, survivors of "the great persecution," sing the praises of the eternal God and the Lamb now permanently in their midst. They are dressed in white robes; the liturgical alb, the white robe often worn by priests and eucharistic ministers in liturgical churches, is a reminder of baptism, and traditional white baptismal robes were in turn a remember of "the white-robed army of martyrs" (from the ancient hymn

---

20. K. Barth, *CD* 1.2, 210.

Riders of the Apocalypse and Other Lurid Scenes (Revelation 4:1–9:21)

Te Deum Laudamus) whose baptism was a baptism of death. Here they proclaim in song the magnificence of God, and of God's eternal provision for the needs of the faithful (Rev 7:16).

As the seventh seal is opened (Rev 8:1) silence descends, for that is what it contains. It provides what I call a "radical caesura" (a literary term for a complete but unexpected break) between the two scenes: "there was silence in heaven for about half an hour." Silence appears elsewhere in the prophetic tradition from which John is borrowing: Hab 2:20 is an unambiguous example, "the Lord is in his holy temple; let all the earth keep silence before him!", but see also Zeph 1:7, "Be silent before the Lord God!" and Zech 2:13, "Be silent, all people, before the Lord; for he has roused himself from his holy dwelling." Something significant is happening here: "For everything there is a season, and a time for every matter under heaven . . . a time to keep silence, and a time to speak" (Eccl 3:1, 7b). In the practice of many non-liturgical churches there is no time for silence: Ps 32:11's "shout for joy, all you upright in heart" has won out over Ps 46:10's "Be still, and know that I am God." There must be room for both. Indeed, since liturgy and worship are our training "on earth as it is in heaven" for John's visualized eternity, it is important to recognize the place for silence in the presence of God, the "still point of a turning world."[21]

> There's a hush of expectation
> and a quiet in the air
> and the breath of God is moving
> in the fervent breath of prayer;
> (from the Hymn "There's a Light Upon the Mountain," Henry Barton)

This radical caesura of silence is a prelude to new explosions of action. Seven angels with their seven trumpets stand poised to liberate vast fields of action. But they must wait. The pause transitions first into the activity which must be the basis of all faith-action, extravagant worship. Worship must *always* be extravagant. In a secular society it is the ultimate waste of time, and therefore in a faith-society it is the ultimate countercultural act (perhaps in the same spirit as the New Age motto "practice random acts of

---

21. From "Burnt Norton" in *T. S. Eliot's* "Four Quartets." Eliot, *Collected Poems*, 179. Helen Gardner notes that the line "is quoted from *Coriolan* I, *Triumphal March*, published in 1931" and that "the image of the dance around the 'still point' was suggested by Charles Williams's novel *The Greater Trumps*, whre in a magical model of the universe the figures of the Tarot pack dance around the Fool at the still centre." Gardner, *Composition*, 85.

kindness"). Miserable worship, in which the candles (if there are any) are burned to the last centimeter, or in which the last drip of eucharistic wine slithers around the lips of the last twenty or so communicants, is anathema. Music should rattle the walls and raise the roof—except when it is quiet and reflective, when it should hang in the air like nightingale song. Gestures should—depending on the surrounds—should be overstated and large, not only to be visible, but to speak of the magnificence of God. Ceremonial garb should hint at the magnificence of heaven (but not the personal whims and fancies of the wearer). It is interesting to note that this eternal worship as witnessed by John begins in silence: the old *Book of Common Prayer* days saw the importance of a reverent approach to worship. John's vision, though, ends in pyrotechnics: it is the Pentecostals who have that right. Our job, as worshipers this side of John's vision, is to rumor that which lies ahead, and we must constantly assess our liturgical practices to see that they are a foretaste of this eschatological liturgy.

Another angel, not one of the seven, censes the altar of God, the smoke rising from his censer uniting with the prayers of the saints to rise before God. I make no secret of my belief that incense is a valuable aid to worship, rising through our earthly sanctuary as a sign and reminder of the great eternal worship of God. By rising, incense symbolizes the movement of prayer into the eternities of God, and its opulent scent represents the very best that we can bring in love and adoration to the one who was and is and is to come. But this worship foreseen by John ends dramatically, as the very coals trigger pyrotechnics and more tectonic upheaval and the pregnant pause in heaven is over.

"Now the seven angels who had the seven trumpets made ready to blow them" (Rev 8:6). The silence and the worship end, and we return to the spine-chilling outpourings across the face of the earth. Again these are the stuff of fear, but they belong not in an arsenal of texts designed to terrify non-believers into the embrace of God, but in an arsenal of images designed to encourage the faithful to remain faithful. The movement of the fire thrown down on earth in Rev 8:5 was a precursor to a series of "flingings" down on earth. The chaos tamed as the first act of creation (Gen 1:2, where the depiction is of a chaotic "formless void," an image picked up again in Jer 4:23) is seemingly to break out once more, as hail and fire and blood descend, and proportions of the earth are destroyed.

It was popular in the millennialist circles of my early Christian faith to see in this imagery a representation of nuclear apocalypse. Certainly,

Riders of the Apocalypse and Other Lurid Scenes (Revelation 4:1–9:21)

as Jürgen Moltmann emphasizes in his writings, since July 16, 1945 (the day when US military scientists exploded a bomb, obscenely called Trinity, in the New Mexico desert), humankind has had the ability to create scenes akin to those depicted in John's vision. That, of course, is why we use the phrase "nuclear holocaust." But John is not predicting Hiroshima, Nagasaki, or some future human cataclysm. Like the contrast between military "shock and awe" and eschatological apocalypse, the contrast between nuclear fission and eschatological apocalypse is no contest. On the other hand, this is not about human happenings: this is about that which we cannot understand, the removal of God's sustaining hand from creation. The imagery of mountains tossed, stars falling, darkness partially covering the sources of celestial light, and the imagery of an eagle heard to speak its brutal message is not like anything humankind can devise. This is the language of the impossible: the Creator is closing creation down.

So, while we may capture some idea of John's vision from a Nagasaki image or from pictures of Vesuvius spewing molten lava, or from the horrific imagery of World Trade Centre towers collapsing or Fukushima swallowed by surges of black unstoppable sea, or by images of the aftermath of the Boxing Day tsunami, we are not speaking of the same thing. The heavenly images of apocalyptic speak of a "like this but so much more" impression of "the heavenly city", while the destructive, chaotic images of apocalyptic speak of a "like this but so much worse." Stinging locusts echo but worsen the destructive plagues of the Pharaoh: indeed, there are many echoes here of the plagues of Egypt (see Exod 9:23), or of Hebrew scriptural scenes of destruction (Ezek 38:22) and the wrath of God. Ultimately all serve as contrast to the scenes of paradise experienced by the saints. John's methodology is simple: take all that is most horrible in your imagination (if you are familiar, as John's audiences were, with the Hebrew Scriptures, allow their darkest images to fill your imagination), and contrast those fear-filled images with the most idyllic and perfected scenes available to your imagination. "Like this but so much worse" is simply contrasted with "like this, but so much more wonderful."

Despite the magnitude of the destruction, earth-bound humanity goes about its business: "they did not repent of their murders or their sorceries or their fornication or their thefts" (Rev 9:21). This is as much as assessment of every era, every present moment, as it is of an eschatological closure. "An evil and adulterous generation asks for a sign, but no sign will be given," says Jesus (Matt 12:39). The dominant belief of the New Testament authors is that we have enough signs; a timeless passage like Rom 1:20–23 or an observation like Rev 9:20 (which could be a direct echo of Rom 1:23) echoes the sentiments of the Psalmist's "The heavens are telling the glory of God, and the firmament proclaims his handiwork" (Ps 19:1) or Ps 8:3–4:

> When I look at your heavens, the work of your fingers,
> the moon and the stars that you have established;
> what are human beings that you are mindful of them,
> mortals that you care for them?

It is an abiding observation, the paradox of what I earlier called "creation theology." The majesty of creation exists, yet humankind is not exactly rushing to enter into the liturgical and sacramental adoration of the Creator. When nature turns and snarls its fury, many who are not willing to believe in a Creator will use the events as an anti-theist argument: how can there be a loving God when tsunamis rage, earthquakes pummel, or cyclones tear humanity from its course? John ends his observations of the fury unleashed by the seven trumpeting angels with a severe observation, yet it could almost be a sigh:

> The rest of humankind, who were not killed by these plagues, did not repent of the works of their hands or give up worshiping demons and idols of gold and silver and bronze and stone and wood, which cannot see or hear or walk. And they did not repent of their murders or their sorceries or their fornication or their thefts (Rev 9:20–21).

He might well be asking himself what sign would in the end convince a people determined not to believe. But in his vision, it is in any case far too late: one third of the earth's population has been destroyed. Lest this seem fanciful, and John's vision appears to be spinning out of control, we should remember that in 437 BCE plague swept through Ethiopia, Egypt, Libya, and Greece, destroying one-third of the known world's population. It is little wonder, that for a moment, we pause when in our modern world a new virus or bacteria makes its presence felt.

4

Shock and Awe (Revelation 10:1–14:20)

FOR THE SECOND TIME (see after Rev 6:17) a sequence of seven portents is interrupted, and the seventh is withheld while a seeming digression in both narrative and action takes place. Before the seventh trumpet sounds, and immediately following the catastrophic liberation of plagues (associated in some circles in the 1980s with HIV/AIDS), John alters his focus to tell of two substantial apparitions. The mediaeval scholars who added chapter divisions to the text accommodated the first of these two apparition-visions in chapter 10, the second in chapter 11.

I suggested in the previous chapter that John, while not engaging in occult or other arcane and Gnostic secrecy, utilized apocalyptic as a form of "open secret" narrative, making his message slightly less accessible to the persecutors of the Christian community, but on the whole accessible to anyone who digs beneath his bizarre (but in fact largely stereotyped) symbolism. There is a considerable contrast between the "closed" secret world of Gnosticism, and the "open" secret of Christian practice—though this is not to say Christians were unaware of Gnostic methods. Biblical scholars will often refer to "Gnosticism"—indeed, there was an era when almost every incomprehensible or mildly baffling New Testament text was dismissed as "gnostic"—as an influence on Christianity and its texts. In fact, the word "Gnosticism" has become so generalized as to be almost meaningless, but, in very loose terms, "Gnosticism" refers to a vast swathe of religious beliefs and practices in the early Christian centuries in which adherents were privy to a certain secret system of "knowledge".[1]

---

1. If you are etymologically inclined you may know the relationship between the

Babylon's Cap

Before the "canon" of Scripture was closed, there were many other Christian writings. Some, as conspiracy theorists delight in telling us, were later suppressed and destroyed by Christian authorities as they strove towards an ultimately unattainable uniformity of Christian doctrine. Amongst those that survive were the delightful if ethereal second-century *Gospel of Thomas* referred to above, and the whimsical *Infancy Gospels of James and Thomas*, from perhaps the third century. There were many that were less well known, such as *The Gospel of Peter* (in which any "bodily" crucifixion of Jesus is denied), *The Gospel according to the Egyptians*, and *The Gospel According to the Hebrews*. Some of these writings were characterized by the assumption that author and audience shared a secret knowledge or *gnosis* unavailable to the outsider. To that extent, Revelation could be termed "gnostic," for it assumes the coding that it uses will be grasped by the audiences of the seven churches (and perhaps beyond). Genuine Gnosticism though, to the extent it can be categorized, saw the knowledge itself as a spark of the divine implanted into the believer. It is possible that the Nicolaitans referred to in the letters to Ephesus and Pergamum were gnostic, but that suggestion is precisely the type of argument from silence. From a lack of concrete evidence, that became a popular form of biblical interpretation in the late nineteenth and twentieth centuries: ultimately we can only guess at the identity of John's internal enemies.

Nevertheless, we need to differentiate emphatically between the arcane systems of knowledge used in Gnostic teachings and the open secrets of John's writing. To his audience, well-versed in Hebrew Scriptures, the image of an angel holding a scroll was always going to be an "Aha!" moment. A comparison from sport may help: in rugby union, the player throwing to the lineout will usually call (or respond to a call) of secret directions. "Four thirteen alpha hippo" will not mean much to the opposition players, but to the well-rehearsed team it will be a clear set of instructions to be followed (if all goes well with the throw!). That is an arcane instruction. On the other hand, as a scrum forms in front of the goal posts, and the backline breaks into a /\-formation with the best kicker in clear space, it will be an open secret that a drop-goal attempt is likely to be taken. That is the "open secret" akin to the revelation symbolism—an "Aha!" moment to those in the know. If you know nothing about rugby you will be in the shoes of many of the Roman authorities, utterly alienated by John's peculiar language.

English, Scandinavian-influenced "kn" construction and the Greek "gn": knowledge = gnowledge!

Shock and Awe (Revelation 10:1–14:20)

So at Rev 10:1 John recounts his vision of "another mighty angel," and his audience says "Aha!" Angels appear in about seventy-five verses in Revelation, including the letters to the churches. References to angels surround the sudden arrival of this "mighty angel," and his arrival from heaven provides an interruption to their narrative. A "mighty angel" appeared in Rev 5:2; in Rev 18:21 an angel will have a "mighty voice." This angel, like that in Rev 5:2, is associated with a scroll, and John's audience would have immediately known not only that the vision was going to build on the earlier scroll of Rev 5:2, but was in some way associated with the angel and scroll of Ezekiel and his prophetic commissioning (Ezek 2:8—3:3). Like Ezekiel, John, is a conveyor of good news and bad—the Christians of Sardis in particular would know which side of that equation they risked ending up on:

> Mortal, I am sending you to the people of Israel, to a nation of rebels who have rebelled against me; they and their ancestors have transgressed against me to this very day. The descendants are impudent and stubborn. I am sending you to them, and you shall say to them, "Thus says the Lord God." Whether they hear or refuse to hear (for they are a rebellious house), they shall know that there has been a prophet among them. And you, O mortal, do not be afraid of them, and do not be afraid of their words, though briers and thorns surround you and you live among scorpions; do not be afraid of their words, and do not be dismayed at their looks, for they are a rebellious house. You shall speak my words to them, whether they hear or refuse to hear; for they are a rebellious house (Ezek 2:3–7).

Until this point, John has not referred back to the seven churches. Now though, to the Sardisians and Laodiceans, there could be little escaping the not-too-subtle warning John delivers. Are they the "rebellious house"? There is much in the vision of John about the coming fate of the external enemies of the church, but there is here a warning to those letting the side down from within: even the sweetness of the scroll is not enough to disguise harsh words of judgment implicit in the message John was about to write down.

However, in a moment not dissimilar to the so-called "messianic secret" moments of Mark's gospel account (e.g., Mark 7:36), John is ordered not to write down, as yet, what he sees. In Mark's account of the Jesus story the messianic secret is designed to ensure that the disciples have the full picture of the extent of divine love before they proclaim the Kingdom. The restraint on John operates at a similar level—the full extent both of the wrath and the mercy of God are yet to be revealed. Nevertheless, this restraint on John operates at another level: he has been given knowledge that remains unavailable to his audience, and he can therefore maintain a degree of prophetic authority or even superiority over them: "I know something you don't know"!

So John is, with an open-secret allusion to Ezekiel, commissioned once more in his bittersweet prophetic task. At the beginning of his *Either/Or*, nineteenth-century philosopher Søren Kierkegaard famously exclaims "What is a poet? An unhappy man who in his heart harbors a deep anguish, but whose lips are so fashioned that the moans and cries which pass over them are transformed into ravishing music."[2] As many, most notably the Welsh priest-poet R. S. Thomas,[3] have noted, prophet and poet stand in the shadow of the same curse. John takes the words given to him by God and reconstructs them for an audience: it is to this task he is recommissioned at Rev 10:11, effectively echoing the words of Jeremiah, "My anguish, my anguish! I writhe in pain!" (Jer 4:19). But now his prophetic language imports a new series of images, as he is sent to observe and measure the Temple and count (the verb "measure" at Rev 11:1 covers both actions, measure and count) its occupants. The scene is based on knowledge of the Jewish Second or Herodian Temple, which was divided into separate courts. The Second Temple contained a court of priests, a court of Israelites, a court of women and an external court of Gentiles, the last effectively a marketplace. The court of Gentiles was separated from the Hebrews' areas by a low barrier, the crossing of which could lead to death for a Gentile.

That much information can be gleaned from history and archaeology, but much of John's symbolism is, perhaps deliberately, obscure. We are, after all, not exactly the audience for which he designed his language, even if we are not the Roman authorities; some aspects of the "line-out call" of his prophecy will escape us. There are clear allusions here to Zechariah's vision in Zech 5:1–2. There the Old Testament prophet, again instructed by an angel, is also confronted by a scroll, a bittersweet curse by which "everyone who steals shall be cut off according to the writing on one side, and everyone who swears falsely shall be cut off according to the writing on the other side" (Zech 5:3). In an earlier part of Zechariah's vision (Zech 4), a lampstand figures, but there are as many differences as there are similarities between John's and Zechariah's vision. John's audience would have heard

---

2. Kierkegaard, *Either/Or*, 20.
3. See his poem "Kierkegaard," R. S. Thomas, *Selected Poems*, 86.

Shock and Awe (Revelation 10:1–14:20)

echoes, too, of Ezekiel's vision in the book of Ezekiel, but there too, while the similarities are striking, the tone and the details are different. Perhaps we are supposed to glean no more than that John is claiming the same prophetic authority as his predecessor.

The command to John to measure the Temple is never fulfilled, as the vision goes on to introduce "two witnesses" (Rev 11:3). The identity of these figures, too, must elude us, though they may have been obvious enough to John's audience. Scholars have speculated as to their identity: ancient interpreters associated them with the patriarchal-prophetic figures Enoch and Elijah, who according to Old Testament narratives were "elevated" into heaven without dying. More modern scholars have proposed that John meant Moses and Elijah. Some scholars, and I tend to agree with this approach, suggest Christian historical figures such as Peter and Paul, or Stephen and James, but each combination presents problems. The reality is we will never establish John's original intention. Instead we must simply recognize these figures as "heroes of faith" in the struggle between good and evil, or more specifically between Christianity and the forces that have from time to time—or at all times, perhaps—opposed it. As an Anglican I might recall the martyred witnesses of the English Reformation, a Nicholas Ridley or a Thomas Cranmer. As moderns we might recall a Dietrich Bonhoeffer or a Martin Luther King. As descendants of the British and Irish heritage, some of us might recall Thomas Becket. All these are witnesses who, like the figures of Rev 11, lived and died for their witness to the Truth. We might recall others, too: missionary Graham Staines, and his sons Philip, 10, and Timothy, 6, who were killed in India's Orissa State as they slept in their jeep in an isolated village, victims of a Hindu militant backlash against Christian mission. And, while the witnesses of Rev 11:3 are eventually killed, it is not necessarily as martyrs that they enter the narrative here: beneficiaries of Anglo-Irish Christianity might recall the feisty abbess, Hilda of Whitby, who had so much beneficial influence on the shape of our traditions.

The authority given to the two witnesses to "shut the sky" is a reminder of the Palestinian origins of our faith narratives, referring back to Elijah (see 1 Kgs 17:1, 18:1). As I have often recounted in the context of baptisms, Australians experience more in common than those in many parts of the world with the Hebrew and other Middle Eastern peoples' sense of connection to water. As Australian capital cities, Darwin excepted, wrestle with questions of the supply and demand of water (and even in Darwin authorities acknowledge the city's phenomenal consumption of water and are currently lifting water rates astronomically), and as acrimonious debates over management of the Murray-Darling Basin refuse to subside, we can well relate to peoples for whom the fear of drought is a bitter economic and social reality. It has often been said that water, not oil, will dwell at the heart of humanity's most bitter battles: the Murray-Darling disputes, for example, are miniscule compared to the tensions over supply, demand, and management of the Nile.

Unlike the Hebrew people, though, the surf-worshipers of Australia and New Zealand do not relate to the great fear of the sea, and all the chaos it represented to the Hebrews. The sea is mentioned in twenty-five verses in Revelation alone, culminating in the telling observations of Rev 20:13 and 21:1. Perhaps, given the obscenely high rate of drowning in both Australia and New Zealand, and following the tsunamis of Boxing Day 2001 and Fukushima 2011, more notice should be taken of the oceans' powerful destructive forces, represented in John's visionary echoes of the Exodus by waters "giving up their dead" or "turning to blood" (cf. Exod 7:14–19, 1 Sam 4:8).

It is in this context that "the beast" so dramatically narrated in popular interpretations and representations of apocalyptic, makes his first appearance. He (can I be sexist in my use of the masculine indefinite pronoun here?) appears without warning as "the beast that comes up from the bottomless pit" (or "abyss," as Aune translates it). Clearly he is a figure known to John's audience, for there is no explanation as to his identity or role. His sole purpose at this moment is to attack and defeat the witnesses, and it is little more than a dark cameo appearance, after which he disappears until Rev 13:10. His brutal conquest here is incomplete, however, for after "three and a half days"—meaning no more than "a proscribed time" again (arguments for echoes of Jesus' period in the tomb are tenuous)—his victims arise, in emulation of the bones of Ezekiel's valley, and are removed to the safety of God's eternities. Hymn-writer Elizabeth Ann Porter Head captures the image both of Ezekiel's valley and of the resuscitation of the witnesses in her hymn "Oh Breath of Life,"

> Oh breath of life come sweeping through us,
> revive your church with life and power;
> O breath of life, come cleanse, renew us,
> and fit your church to meet this hour.

In this case, though, the witnesses have borne more than adequate testimony to their faith, and are removed from battle.

Shock and Awe (Revelation 10:1–14:20)

The perspective of Revelation always transcends death. The death of witnesses represented by these two apocalyptic figures in Rev 11 is no less a death than yours or mine, and clearly no less bloody a death than that of Jesus, or of a Peter or a Paul, a Thomas Becket or a Graham, Philip or Timothy Staines. Christianity is not a denial of death, but a denial of the finality of death. We will die, but unlike the bleak vision of Job 7:6, "My days are swifter than a weaver's shuttle, and come to their end without hope", we will die in what the author of Hebrews calls "a hope that enters the inner shrine behind the curtain" (Heb 6:19, cf. Eph 2:12). This is a fundamental perspective of apocalyptic, and John represents it in a brief vignette of the two witnesses. Their death, left to "lie in the street of the great city that is prophetically called Sodom and Egypt, where also their Lord was crucified" (Rev 11:8) is a brutal death, giving cause for that most subhuman of responses, dancing and celebration by the victims' enemies. Leaving a body unburied is an act of contempt (Ps 79:2). Dancing on metaphorical or actual graves is never less than obscenity. However understandable might be the glee of many Libyans at the death of Muammar Gaddafi, Iraqis at the death of Saddam Hussein, or Romanians at the death of Nicolai Ceausescu, celebration of a person's death is always one of the most visceral and demeaning of human actions. In this visionary scene it is the death of righteous martyrs that is celebrated (as it often has been), significantly in the city where their Lord was crucified (Rev 11:8b). But now, in John's hands, that city is not merely a geographical location, but the "earthly city" of all human existence.

The response of the crowds to the martyrs' death is an orgy of rejoicing. The martyrs had discomforted the populace, rattling the coziness of their complacency, as prophets always will ("the upright are an abomination to the wicked," according to Prov 29:27). The crowds' response to the martyrs' resuscitation is terror. Unusually in Revelation, terror is expressed by giving glory to God—by an act of worship, which is the desired response of humanity to their encounter with God ("what is the chief end of man? To glorify God and to enjoy him for ever," as The Westminster Confession expresses it). This response of awe-filled terror, though, is elicited only after catastrophic portents.

The Old Testament notion of a remnant surviving is here deliberately and darkly reversed, and a similar remnant is instead killed. Earthquakes appear several times in Revelation, and they are both an allusion to the epoch-ending earthquake of Matt 27:51, and, as previously suggested, to one of nature's most terrifying and inescapable phenomena. A death toll of 7,000 is not large when measured against standards of earthquake destruction, but it probably should be understood as a "fore-ordained" or "prescribed number" (see 1 Kgs 19:18). This awe and glorification of God is elicited by duress: if this is indeed an image of the conversions of nations, it may well throw up a question or two about the much-loved evangelical emphasis on freedom of will!

John was not a modern writer working with an editorial team: just as the Temple is never actually measured, despite the command of Rev 11:1–2, so the third woe is never recounted. This small detail should warn us against too literalistic an interpretation of John or indeed any biblical writer. The Scriptures were written (and subsequently transcribed) under enormous social and psychological pressure, and the degree to which they are coherent is miraculous. The awaited third woe does not eventuate, lost in John's bigger vision. He moves instead to the delayed seventh trumpet blast (and the end of the second caesura), which is accompanied by a heavenly hymn.

This hymn (Rev 11:15b–18) is a celebration of the extraordinary acts of God: the dead are judged, the righteous rewarded, the wicked punished. It is an enactment or even a demonstration of the decision in Rev 11:13 to give glory to God, to become what I call a eucharistic people. This motif of giving thanks, or "glory" as the NRSV puts it, appears frequently in different forms throughout both the Hebrew and Christian Scriptures, and it is not one to be glossed over. John has alluded to the Old Testament notion of "remnant" in the preceding sentences, a notion which appears no fewer than seventy times in the Hebrew Scriptures (see, e.g., Mic 5:7). In John's vision, a tenth of the city—representative of all humanity—are killed, and the remainder, effectively coerced in shock, finally give the appropriate glory to God. The more common pattern, however, is for a remnant to remain after a punitive action of God. This is at least in part the point of John's reference to 1 Kgs 19:18, although his reversal of proportions may hint that John is not prepared to limit the magnitude of divine grace even under apocalyptic duress.

Frequently the Scriptures allude to God's people as a "priestly people," Exod 19:6 being the formative reference. The notion is borrowed from the creation narrative's depiction of God's placement of humans on earth to "care for and husband" (Gen 1:28)[4] the earth and all that is in it. The psalms

---

4. The traditional word "subdue" had been tragically abused in Christian history, and is a distortion of the Hebrew. A more modern translation such as the *Contemporary*

take this idea and develop it further so that human beings have the role of voicing the vast range of human and even nature's experience, as is particularly apparent in Psalms 148—150. The underlying theological idea, then, is that human beings are the priests of creation, giving praise because creation otherwise has no voice: "As God's gifts, all his creatures are fundamentally eucharistic beings also; but the human being is able—and designated—to express the praise of all created things before God."[5]

This priestly theme is picked up in the *Benedicite* tradition, the "Song of the Three."[6] The Song of the Three is deliberately based on the ethos of Ps 150, as well as a long passage from Daniel 3, generally omitted, after verse 23. The latter passage was not considered by the reformers to be authentically Danielic, and was omitted from Protestant Bibles or relegated to secondary status as "Apocrypha" or "deuterocanonical." It is considered canonical by the Roman Catholic and Eastern Orthodox traditions (it appears in italics in *The New Jerusalem Bible*), and is acknowledged in the 39 Articles of the Anglican tradition as to be "read for example of life and instructions of manners" but not to "establish any doctrine" (Article 6).

John predates these Reformation subtleties, but he would have been well aware of a theology of vicarious prayer, singing the praise of creation (Ps 150). He would have been aware, too, of the remnant-strand in writings and oral traditions contemporary to him. Those traditions, breaking from time to time to the surface of our New Testament texts, draw from an overview of human history. Humankind, along with all creation, was pronounced "good" by the Creator, but humanity, according to the Genesis tradition, fell—our behavior since crawling out of the primeval swamp suggests the Genesis authors were well-versed in human conduct! Subsequently, only a remnant, the Hebrew people, was called into priestly relationship with God. They in turn were represented in approach to God by a caste of priests, who had to undergo much ritual purification in order to draw near to God, and above all by a high priest. To the Christian community, Jesus himself took over the role of the high priest (see especially the book of Hebrews), but the Jesus community was nevertheless commissioned to give thanks—or make eucharist, as I will often call it—in all circumstances (e.g.,

---

English Version does little better with "control". Sadly the word "husband" is also tainted by centuries of domestic abuse and oppression, but the verb should be understood in its original egalitarian meaning, not seen through the prisms of oppression or abuse.

5. Moltmann, *God in Creation*, 71.

6. See *A Prayer Book for Australia*, 399, or *A New Zealand Prayer Book / He Karakia Mihinare o Aotearoa*, 102.

1 Thess 5:18, Eph 5:20). The Lukan story of the ten lepers (Luke 17:11–19) picks up this imagery in a particularly striking way: all ten are met in their basic human need of wholeness ("he makes his sun rise on the evil and on the good, and sends rain on the righteous and on the unrighteous" according to Matt 5:45), but only one returns to "give thanks" (make eucharist).

John reflects this idea in Rev 11:15–18, as he depicts not specific numbers of "the saved" but a generalized number who are awestruck by the acts of God, repent from godlessness, and turn instead to give glory. Thus, from the earthquake an explosion of eucharistic praise bursts forth, in a form not dissimilar to the Great Prayer of Thanksgiving in the subsequent eucharistic liturgies of the liturgical Christian community. Like our eucharistic prayers, this generalized song of the saints at worship can only be representative, not exhaustive, in declaring the acts of God in and around cosmic history. John might sympathize with the gospel-author, his namesake: "Now Jesus did many other signs in the presence of his disciples, which are not written in this book" (John 20:30), and "there are also many other things that Jesus did; if every one of them were written down, I suppose that the world itself could not contain the books that would be written" (John 21:25). So deep is this hymn of praise in Revelation that nature itself joins in (Rev 11:19).

Suddenly John's scene shifts. The narrative of the pregnant woman is deeply disturbing, and we should not deny its discomfort. Women, not least pregnant women, have always been utterly vulnerable in the context of war, as Jesus himself alludes in his apocalyptic discourse (Matt 24:19). This apocalyptic portent is in fact visualized as a cosmic constellation—a reminder that, while the popular astrological platitudes of daily newspapers and weekly magazines are vacuous, ancient societies, not least Aboriginal societies, turned to the heavens and found great wisdom there. The Bible itself is gloriously ambivalent on the subject, though the rule of thumb should be "does this practice point to or away from the Creator?" Compare Isa 47:13–17 with the un-condemned practice of the Magi in Matt 2:1–2, for example, and the ambivalence is apparent. While this may seem a digression, it is an important reminder that the practices of ancient cultures, not least the Dreamtime, should not be dismissed out of hand.

A sign, comprehensible to those who see it, is witnessed in the heavens—we need to be sensible in response to this, for sometimes a comet is just a comet. Bishop Bruce Wilson writes about his own private "theophany experience" whilst enthroned on an outside dunny in a working-class inner-Sydney suburb. Questioning what he should do after leaving school,

Shock and Awe (Revelation 10:1–14:20)

he mused on the loo, and "an unusual event occurred. I saw a meteorite flash across the sky. I recall thinking 'I've been sitting here most nights for years and that's the first time I've seen a meteorite.'" On the following night Wilson experienced a repetition of the event: "Years and years and never a one, now a meteorite two nights running." He adds. "I confess I did ask myself if this was some kind of a sign, whether there was any meaning to it." The same scene occurred on the third successive night. As time and reflections went on, Wilson took these events as a "sign" he should enter the priesthood. He concludes his narrative wisely:

> For a few weeks—and take into account I was only seventeen at the time—I entertained the idea that God had intentionally "flicked" those meteorites across the sky for me. A miracle! It is a story capable of such dramatic interpretation.
>
> I soon learnt from an astronomy text that it was the usual time of the year for meteorite showers. I accepted that the meteorites were not "sent" for me. But the conviction that this was, nevertheless, a theophany (a word I had not heard of then) remained. I continued to accept that the totality of the experience constituted my "call" to serve God in the ministry of the church.[7]

God, the God of heavens and earth, finds highly individualized means by which to communicate to us. Once more: the litmus test is does this experience point to what Paul calls "Christ and him crucified"? Does this experience serve the gospel?

The pregnant woman of John's vision is a timeless portent—not to be confused with some historical figure or event (the formation of the European Economic Community [EEC] was a popular interpretation in millennialist circles in the late 1970s). Images of the gestation of a child as symbolizing an action of God are common in the Hebrew Scriptures.[8] Like the two witnesses of the preceding chapter, she could be and has been interpreted in many ways: was she Mary? The church? The persecuted people of God? More important than her identity, though, is her authority: even the zodiac (the twelve stars of Rev 12:1)[9] is subject to her. She was a sign. The word for "sign," *semeion*, is critical to both New Testament Johns, appearing seventeen times in the Fourth Gospel and four in Revelation. The author of

---

7. Wilson, *Reasons*, 9–10.

8. Isa 7:14—cf. for example 1 Thess 5:3—and 13:8, 21:3, 26:12, 42:14; Jer 4:31, 6:24, 13:21, 22:23, 30:6, 49:24, 50:43; Mic 4:9; Ps 48:7.

9. See J. Massyngberde Ford, *Revelation*, 189.

2 Thess is more skeptical: "The coming of the lawless one is apparent in the working of Satan, who uses all power, signs, lying wonders" (2 Thess 2:9), and Luke and Matthew record sayings that suggest Jesus was very cautious about signs: "An evil and adulterous generation asks for a sign, but no sign will be given to it except the sign of the prophet Jonah" (a reference to his own death and resurrection: Matt 12:39). Jesus' concern, though, provides an important underscoring of my own dictum: does this "sign" point to Jesus and his cross, and the proclamation of it?

Perhaps Jesus' own caution about signs was due to their ambivalence. To every interpretation there is an equal and opposite counter-interpretation! Immediately in the heavens there is a counter-sign. The word dragon (*drakōn*) appears only in Revelation in the New Testament, but it appears there thirteen times. Draco, in its Anglicized form, after whom, presumably, Draco Malfoy in *Harry Potter* is named, is a conspicuous constellation in the northern skies, and has been recognized as such since the time of Ptolemy—the time of John. Draco was soon associated by Christians with the serpent that tempted Eve in the Garden of Eden, as is suggested by the slightly awkward scene and comment at Rev 12:7–9.

This heavenly dragon sets up an evil counterpoint to the figure of the woman. With characteristic draconian arrogance, the figure destroys one-third of the universe (based on Dan 8:10), but it is not this show of strength that is his most terrifying potential for John's audience. His reference to gestation and to the vulnerability of pregnancy will have already alerted them to his intention of paralleling (juxtaposing) Christ's salvation with the powers of evil, and the image of the dragon hovering in readiness to devour a Christ-figure is an unnerving one. It is of course also a bizarre one—Christ has long since been incarnated in and from the womb of Mary, but the audience is expected to know that there a sense in which the church as well as Mary gestate the Savior, and that it is in this capacity that Christ's work is vulnerable in the apocalyptic end time. The images are complex and do not automatically translate into the audience's reality: the Mary/church figure is "snatched away into the wilderness," as Jesus was following his baptism, while her infant is carried off into heaven (John has probably intertwined different materials, and the constellation-woman is now firmly placed on earth). The wilderness is almost always in the Judeo-Christian world view a place of prayer and of encounter with God, and it is on prayer that the church must rely if it is to persevere.

Shock and Awe (Revelation 10:1–14:20)

There "she can be nourished for one thousand two hundred and sixty days" (Rev 12:6). John plays frequently with this figure, and it appears in various forms: as forty-two months and as three and a half years, three and a half being half of seven's perfection. Despite a loose appearance of chronological accuracy the figure in all its forms simply once more denotes "a divinely restricted period,"[10] and is an echo of Daniel's "a time, two times, and half a time" (Dan 7:25). It should be read as a period of non-specific duration, but a period in the hands of God. Historically, however, three and a half years (roughly) elapsed between the beginnings of the Jewish revolt and the siege of Jerusalem.

The slightly awkward insertion of a minor third narrative, as Michael and his angels fight the dragon and his minions in heaven, ends, as it must (because these scenes are all declarations of faith in a God who is in control) in the defeat and expulsion of the dragon, and he is "thrown down" to earth. Presumably he had been visiting heaven in his search for the child. This has been "warfare in heaven itself,"[11] not in the immediate realms of human experience. Michael appears in Dan 12:1, in some bodies of intertestamental literature,[12] and in Jude 9, effectively as a lieutenant-general figure in the armies of the Christ. Here his victory leads to another outburst of eucharistic praise (Rev 12:10–12), and the thwarted dragon turns his attention back to the formerly gestating woman and her allies. This brief reference may have served to remind John's audience of the cause of their current heightened suffering, as the dragon turned to maraud the woman and her other offspring, "those who keep the commandments of God and hold the testimony of Jesus" (Rev 12:17).

The dragon retreats from center stage, and a new symbol of evil arises. John is turning to focus on scenes of the enemies of Christ's people, and the dragon gives way for a return appearance of the beast. In Dan 7:1–8, itself an allusion to the Leviathan in Ps 74:14 and elsewhere, the sea monster represented hostile foreign nations, whether generalized or specific; it is possible therefore that there is here a veiled allusion to the newly appointed Roman governor in Asia Minor, who arrived by sea each year to rule the province with Caesar's iron rod. But there is no need for specifics,

---

10. Aune, *Revelation 6–16*, 609.
11. Mounce, *Revelation*, 235.
12. A similar figure appears in the intertestamental literature that influenced John: see 1 En 90:14, Charlesworth, *Apocalyptic*, 70. Cf. the *Testament of Dan* 6.2: Charlesworth, *Apocalyptic*, 810. Both are from (approximately) the second century BCE.

and this Leviathan, empowered by the dragon (Rev 3:2), with its catena of blasphemy (Rev 3:5), is a representation of all tyrannical leaders.

A problem with the somewhat puerile attempts of millennialists in comfortable Western cultures to play games with the identities of "beast," "dragon," and other apocalyptic figures is that to do so is to belittle the genuine suffering of those who are oppressed by tyrannical leaders. Henry Kissinger may have been many things, but he was not a dictatorial oppressor. My ironic labeling of Rob Muldoon as an alternative beast, never intended to be serious, points to the risk of trivialization: Muldoon was a take-no-prisoners leader, but he was a leader in a democratic nation, and was eventually rolled by the opposition Labour Party led by David Lange. There are more genuinely draconian figures in the world, and we do not need to find ways by which to make the letters of their name add up to 666 in order to identify them as "anti-Christ," antagonistic to all that Christ represents. Could we make suggestions today? Standing up for Christlike values of justice and compassion in Frank Bainimarama's Fiji is no easy task, though one may survive, albeit bloodied and bruised. Standing up against the Indonesian government, striving for Christlike values of justice and compassion and rights to land in West Papua, can well prove fatal. Standing up against the tyrannies of Robert Mugabe in Zimbabwe is unlikely to provide a long-term future of health and well-being: Burma, Saudi Arabia, Syria, Yemen—there is a long list of nations in which freedom of speech, the first victim of oppression, is only a distant memory, though the geo-political map is ever-changing.

Neither do we need to look that far afield to find histories of tyranny. Telling the story of the decimation of the Yolŋu people in the Northern Territory, Richard Trudgen narrates a powerful moment of oppression, as the Balanda ("European" in Yolŋu languages) stockmen used Murri mercenaries to victimize the Yolŋu:

> Travelling with these Balanda stockmen was a "part-colored" Aboriginal man whom the Yolŋu understood to be a Murri (a Queensland Aboriginal). He was the one used by the Balanda to befriend the southern Arnhem Land clans. He learned some of their language and lived with them at the cattle station. This Murri was the Yolŋu "ganger" or leader. He was at the first shooting [of Yolŋu] and actually took part in it. He immediately turned to the Yolŋu who were with the stockmen and said, "That's the way it is. You have to follow us now, or you will get killed by your own people."[13]

13. Trudgen, *Warriors*, 21.

Shock and Awe (Revelation 10:1–14:20)

A hallmark of tyranny, skillfully utilized by the Romans long before the British, is to pit traitors from within a conquered people against their neighbor, enforcing the rule of new law, a pattern of divide and conquer. It was a model Jesus foretold in one of his own apocalyptic warnings:

> See, I am sending you out like sheep into the midst of wolves; so be wise as serpents and innocent as doves. Beware of them, for they will hand you over to councils and flog you in their synagogues; and you will be dragged before governors and kings because of me, as a testimony to them and the Gentiles. When they hand you over, do not worry about how you are to speak or what you are to say; for what you are to say will be given to you at that time; for it is not you who speak, but the Spirit of your Father speaking through you. Brother will betray brother to death, and a father his child, and children will rise against parents and have them put to death; and you will be hated by all because of my name. But the one who endures to the end will be saved. When they persecute you in one town, flee to the next; for truly I tell you, you will not have gone through all the towns of Israel before the Son of Man comes (Matt 10:16–23).

Jeremiah, too, saw it with a heavy heart: "Slaves rule over us; there is no one to deliver us from their hand" (Lam 5:8).

John's vision now becomes a roll call of evil, as "a second beast," rising this time from the earth (the mechanics are unimportant), begins his rule of terror over "every tribe and people and language and nation," longhand for the known world. Again, it is not necessary to identify historic figures, as in any case tyrant will often supplant tyrant ("a Mirabeau led inexorably to a Robespierre":[14] Vladimir Lenin was succeeded by Joseph Stalin, George Speight, who ousted democratically elected Mahendra Chaudhry, was replaced by a Bainimarama . . . in 69 CE there were no fewer than four dictatorial and tyrannical Caesars in murderous succession!). Like all good tyrants, this second beast seizes control of the commercial markets and makes absolute obedience to his tyranny a prerequisite for trade—a ploy well known to Robert Mugabe. There were suggestions in the late 1970s that the establishment of the EEC, a trading market originally incorporating six nations but soon growing to nine, was the ten horns of the beast. Like many conspiracy theories, this suggestion had a loose attachment to reality, as the proposed European Union was a trading concept, but for all its imperfections it was no dictatorship. Speculation reached fever pitch when Greece

---

14. Kreider, "Way of Christ," 54. See above.

joined the market in 1981, creating a ten-horned beast. Unfortunately for the doomsayers Greenland later left, and the number never returned to ten, as Spain and Portugal joined simultaneously the following year.

But complacency will often breed apocalyptic speculation. The message of John is reiterated once more: endure, for God is in control. This new beast is depicted as a "false prophet," a Behemoth-figure, to be interpreted through the lens of Job 40:15. The Behemoth is a male, counterpoint to the feminine Leviathan of the preceding scene, but there is no need to look for a Margaret Thatcher, Helen Clark, Julia Gillard or Angela Merkel to find historical figures who have practiced "misleading of the saints." It is probable that this is a fifth column figure in John's understanding, operating ostensibly from within a faith community in order to lead the faithful from the path of truth. If the Yolŋu people encountered irresistible force in the waves of Balanda[15] conquest, this enemy is more subtle, applying charlatanism as its primary weapon. I referred in my introduction to the charlatanism of Harold Camping, whose doomsday predictions culminated in the non-return of Jesus on October 21, 2011, but who raised in excess of US$100 million in the lead up to his predicted *parousia*. However bizarre Camping's predictions may have seemed to many of us, the deceitful hermeneutical methodology used in producing his own zany interpretations for his uncritical millennialist Christian audiences is more akin to John's second beast than to the wholesale debilitation experienced by those on the receiving end of Balanda's attacks or those of Mugabe's strongmen. There is, nevertheless, a dark underside to idiocy.

In The Mortal Instruments series of teen fantasy literature written by Cassandra Clare, the primary villain is an attractive and seductive character by the name of Valentine Morgenstern. His Hitlerian passion for purity utterly convinces those who come under his aegis, and they are swept aside by his charisma. The name "Morgenstern," of course, is a reference to "Morning Star," a title for Jesus in Rev 22:16, but it is also a title frequently ascribed to Satan, as the Greek "phosphorous" is translated "Lucifer" in Latin. Morgenstern believes that he has been called to a superhuman crusade to purify

---

15. "Balanda" is a Yolŋu matha [language] word; in south and south-western Australia, for example, the Nyungar people use the term "wedjela" as a rendition of "white fella." Māori use "pakeha." Each is, as I understand it, not technically a definition of ethnicity, much less skin colour, but of "otherness." I use the Yolŋu matha word as I am writing in traditionally Yolŋu lands. Perhaps the most chilling alternative is the word "Nowhummoe," used by the Pennemekeer people of north-west Tasmania, translatable as "devil." See Ryan, *Tasmanian Aborigines*, 167.

Shock and Awe (Revelation 10:1–14:20)

humanity.[16] The echoes of Nietzsche's writings, which strongly influenced Adolf Hitler's ideology, are all too obvious. In 1878 Nietzsche wrote "In all great deceivers a remarkable process is at work to which they owe their power. In the very act of deception with all its preparations . . . they are overcome by their belief in themselves; it is this belief which then speaks, so persuasively, so miracle like, to the audience."[17] One observer notes, "Hitler not only gave his audience reassurance and hope, but received back renewal of his confidence and confirmation of his own self-image."[18]

In another teen fantasy series, the dystopic novels of the Chaos Walking series, the author Patrick Ness reflects on the extent to which a reasonably rational observer can be seduced by evil: "Until there's war, we are only children."[19] The desire to "prove" himself almost leads the central character to allow himself to be caught up in the villain's racial purification programs. Whether it be a fictional character, such as Clare's Morgenstern or Ness's Mayor, or a minor religious or other public persuader, such as Camping, or a major destructive political or religious egotist, the process is the same: a symbiotic relationship develops between orator and audience which leads to the displacement of standards of human decency or common sense, and which can lead to a disaster as (comparatively) minor as Camping's millennialist lunacy, as catastrophic as Jones's or Koresh's quasi-religious cultic practices, or as globally evil as Hitler's or Stalin's pogroms.

It is the subtle distorters of truth who are the most dangerous, as the author of 2 Peter recognizes: "Even so, many will follow their licentious ways, and because of these teachers the way of truth will be maligned. And in their greed they will exploit you with deceptive words. Their condemnation, pronounced against them long ago, has not been idle, and their destruction is not asleep" (2 Pet 2:2–3).

It was easy as a child growing up in the sixties and seventies to see Adolf Hitler as something of an idiotic buffoon, mustachioed and Chaplinesque (Charlie Chaplin, of course, utilized the similarities to subversive

---

16. See Clare, *Ashes*, 244–5; Clare, *Bones*, 401. Another masterful portrayal of evil in its form of obsession with so-called "racial purity" is that of Professor Umbridge in Rowling, *Phoenix*.

17. From Nietzsche's *Human, All Too Human*, published in 1878. Paragraph 52. This is available online at http://nietzsche.holtof.com/Nietzsche_human_all_too_human/sect2_on_the_History_of_Moral_Feelings.htm

18. Bullock, *Hitler and Stalin*, 398.

19. Ness, *Monsters*, 11.

effect).[20] It was not until I began reading the theology of Jürgen Moltmann that I realized how seductive Hitler's policies were to a nation impoverished by the economic strictures placed on it following the Kaiser's war. It can be terribly convincing to expostulate that "our country is at stake," while denigrating a group within society who are defined by race or another cultural construct. When John Howard infamously utilized Geoffrey Blainey's phrase "a black arm-band view of history" in order to dismiss the claims of Indigenous Australians to special consideration, he was attempting to silence the voice of Australia's most vulnerable ethnic group. In doing so he was playing loose with the harsh realities of life on the wrong side of the socioeconomic scales. Unfortunately such populist catchcries distort truth, and truth is the first victim not only of civil warfare but of the self-preserving battles of those whose interest lies in the status quo.[21]

Any fundamentalist reading of the book of Revelation, incidentally, should probably be excluded by a close reading of Rev 13:11: "it had two horns like a lamb" is a mistake unlikely to be repeated by a farmer! This in itself should serve as a warning against speculative readings of the climactic statement "let anyone with understanding calculate the number of the beast, for it is the number of a person. Its number is six hundred sixty-six" (Rev 13:18). John has narrated an accumulative vision of evil—or a vision of accumulative evil—and the Mark of the Beast, the imperfection or anti-perfection of 666, will be repeated wherever and whenever tyrannical and oppressive forces counter the gospel of Jesus Christ, whether by subtlety or by force. John's solution dwells firmly in a doctrine of tenacious perseverance (Rev 13:10):

> Divine protection is the basis for real security and self-worth. There is no human nurture that can ultimately be relied upon or any defensive strategy that will ultimately protect. To be secure in oneself is to be secure in God and to accept oneself as worthy and glorious in the sight of God; to accept that we are loved even if we are not able to feel it. That is no easy task, but it is the root of a sense of worth that does not have to rely on the ephemeral nature

---

20. My friend and colleague Christopher Honoré, in reviewing this study, rightly reminded me that to those born in the late forties and early fifties, images of Hitler have an entirely different, more chilling impact. It would be interesting to enquire of each generation their feelings associated with an image of Hitler.

21. The National Rifle Association in the US uses similar tactics to maintain their interpretation of the Second Amendment in support of citizens' rights to own assault weapons.

Shock and Awe (Revelation 10:1–14:20)

of false gods, which, as Revelation reminds us, ultimately involve us in the worship of the beast.[22]

Or, from the same commentator,

> Revelation's advice to its readers is not a defensiveness based on weapons of war or protection of oneself, but an admonition to continue the way of the testimony of Jesus. There is no guarantee that there will be no threat or freedom from threat or harm. Nevertheless, the reality of the threat is nothing compared to the nakedness that is exposed at the judgment of Christ and the impoverishment of one's own integrity by the (apparently sensible) strategy of self-protection through wealth, property, and accommodation with the beast."[23]

John is ultimately a purveyor of good news, not of doom, and he will always juxtapose evil with conquering goodness.

In chapter 14 John changes tone, and he visualizes the great conquest of Christ and his angels over the demonic forces. This is the first time we have seen the Lamb since Rev 6:1, and he is accompanied now by his 144,000 chaste followers. Sexuality has often been seen with distrust in the Judaeo-Christian (and indeed, Islamic) tradition as a distraction from the "main game" of service of God, and as a distraction from purity. Bodily functions were viewed with distrust, and bodily fluids were seen as distasteful (Lev15:31–32). We cannot rewrite the texts of our forebears, but we could perhaps strive for a more inclusive vision. We have, mainly since the explosion of HIV/AIDS on the international scene in the 1980s, recognized the power of bodily fluids as transporters of life and death, and there is good in that recognition. We must not, however, demonize women (or those who are HIV-positive), and we can refrain from doing so in this context by recognizing the 144,000 as metaphorically rather than sexually chaste. Again we may think of those whose lives of commitment to Godly values—values of the reign of justice and love—bear witness to the coming reign of God: a Desmond Tutu, or the Balanda missionaries who risked their lives, standing between the hunters' guns and the Aboriginal people of Arnhem Land. These are what we might consider the "spiritual athletes," and today we may not necessarily associate athleticism with celibacy, though there remain some for whom celibacy is a life choice.

---

22. Rowland, "Revelation," 652.
23. Ibid.

Babylon's Cap

As John's view changes to the victor's camp, he waxes so eloquently that he loses control of his terminology, celebrating (in Greek) the vision of "harpers harping on on their harps"! It is a lovely image, and John can be excused for allowing, momentarily, his prose to run away, for he does so as he extols the glorious victory of Christ over evil. John himself acknowledges that he cannot convey the magnificence of the victors' song (Rev 14:3, cf. 2 Cor 12:4), and he admits that he himself is not one of the 144,000. This admission grants hope and encouragement to the more flawed amongst us. He cites a vision of angels evangelizing (proclaiming) to every nation, a reminder to us that at no time does John attempt to define who are "the saved." The message of the first angel in this vision is simple: "Fear God and give him glory" (Rev 14:7). This is once more a call to become what I described earlier as "the tenth leper" (see Luke 17:10–19), a people of thanksgiving to the God in whom there is hope against all evil. The second angel provides cause for celebration: Babylon is fallen.

At last we have the first mention of Babylon in the book of Revelation. Borrowed from the book of Daniel, Babylon is simply metonymy (a word picture) for Rome, the tyrannical power oppressing the people of God. When Daniel voiced his prophecies, Babylon was the Neo-Babylonian Empire, and Nebuchadnezzar its king. John utilized the same method. Babylon and Rome alike conquered swathes of territory, oppressing or slaughtering all resistance, and brooking no internal opposition. It was apocalyptic scholar Richard Bauckham who most clearly expressed the implications of this shifting imagery: "Any society whom Babylon's cap fits must wear it. Any society which absolutizes its own economic prosperity at the expense of others" comes under Babylon's condemnation."[24] Were I standing in the shoes of Yolŋu people, I would, with good reason, see the Balanda empire as Babylon, destroying my culture, my law, and my people. Were I an Anglican Christian in Mugabe's Zimbabwe, I might well see Mugabe and his empire as Babylon, as he seized my churches and replaced my clergy with others loyal to his regime.

While genuine democracy (as against, for example, Vladimir Putin's version of it) is a reasonable check and balance against the formation of the modern equivalent of the Babylonian Empire, we might raise one question about the financial and military powerhouse that is the US. As George W. Bush's war machine prepared to move into Afghanistan, Bush proclaimed "I'm the commander in chief, see, I don't need to explain, I do not need

---

24. Bauckham, *Theology*, 156.

Shock and Awe (Revelation 10:1–14:20)

to explain why I say things. That's the interesting part about being president. Maybe somebody needs to explain to me why they say something, but I don't feel like I owe anybody an explanation."[25] Internally the US is a democracy, but its response to the demands of the United Nations (UN)—for example, with regards to Guantanamo Bay, Iraq, and the incursion of Iranian and Pakistani air space with spy drones—suggests that it does not see itself as answerable to other nations. It will of course argue that many of the nations to which the UN demands it be answerable are themselves tyrannies, and it may be right. Babylon's cap does not quite fit the US, but its leadership must constantly evaluate its role in world politics with a harsh and even biblical critical eye.

Bravely John depicts the second angel predicting the fall of Babylon-Rome (Rev 14:8). John was writing at the height of the Roman Empire, when the Caesar, despite fierce struggles and transitions of power, was ruler of the (known) world. It was more inconceivable that Rome would fall than would be the concept of the fall of the US today. John was not a soothsayer: in retrospect we can see that the Roman Empire, like all human empires, eventually gave way, in its western branch, to the conquest of German king Odoacer in 474 CE. Its western branch (for it finally split in two in 395 CE) struggled on until the Ottoman Turks conquered Constantinople in 1453 CE.

Did John foresee these events? No. John was not a clairvoyant, but a seer in the prophetic tradition. If we take a literal approach to his prescience we would have to acknowledge that, though his Babylon has fallen, the millennia of peace of Revelation 20 has never been fulfilled. This might of course indicate that the events he narrated remain yet to be fulfilled, that Rome was not his Babylon, and that his and Ronald Reagan's Armageddon still lies ahead of us. The fact is it does: for as long as humanity exists there will be Babylons, and for longer than humanity exists in its present, flawed form there will be the victory of Christ. Deeply penetrated in all his being by his faith in the risen, death-conquering Christ, John saw and knew that tyranny will not and can never have the final word.

The third angel in Rev 14:9 takes us back to the charlatan faith leaders of chapter 13, and their destruction. Again there need be no suggestion here that a Harold Camping is condemned to some eternal fires of hell: misguided, yes, and therefore marked with the beastly mark of failure, yes.

---

25. Cited in Woodward, *Bush at War*, 145–46.

Babylon's Cap

But there but by the grace go I: it is our role as readers of John's apocalyptic vision to pray that we do not fall:[26]

> But you, beloved, build yourselves up on your most holy faith; pray in the Holy Spirit; keep yourselves in the love of God; look forward to the mercy of our Lord Jesus Christ that leads to eternal life. And have mercy on some who are wavering; save others by snatching them out of the fire (Jude 20–23a).

It is my own belief that even for a Jim Jones, and of course his victims, there can be a word of hope: "For God has imprisoned all in disobedience so that he may be merciful to all. O the depth of the riches and wisdom and knowledge of God! How unsearchable are his judgments and how inscrutable his ways!" (Rom 11:32–33). But the interpretation of this dimension of salvation belongs elsewhere: I shall return to it.

John repeats his call for endurance (Rev 14:12), and to "hold fast to the faith of" or to "faith in" (the Greek is the same) Jesus. It is repeated over and again in Revelation because it is the kernel of John's message. Scholars expend a lot of ink over the question of "faith of Jesus" *vis-à-vis* "faith in Jesus" in this context, and even more in Galatians (Gal 2:16, 3:22) and Romans (Rom 3:22, 3:26). I was recently at a dinner table conversation in which a priest stated categorically that anyone who believed Paul or John was referring to salvation by "the faith of Jesus Christ" was "just stupid." As is so often the case, I was too astounded to remonstrate, and the conversation flowed on while I sat opening and closing my mouth aimlessly. For some, particularly those of a fiercely evangelical tradition (my interlocutor was a graduate of Moore College), there is a fear that translating the ambiguous phrase as salvation "by the faith *of* Jesus" removes responsibility for a personal decision for and conversion to Jesus. The argument is, frankly, fatuous. Regardless of the call to a personal decision to follow Christ, there can be no decision to adopt faith *in* Jesus without the prior event of the faith *of* Jesus. It is certain that Paul and John alike were aware of the ambivalent nuances of their language, and quite simply meant both.

John concludes this passage of celebration of celestial victory with an allusion to Dan 7:13:

> I saw one like a human being
> coming with the clouds of heaven.
> And he came to the Ancient One
> and was presented before him.

---

26. See Mark 13:14–23; Luke 17:23–24, 37; 21:20–24.

Shock and Awe (Revelation 10:1–14:20)

> To him was given dominion
> and glory and kingship,
> that all peoples, nations, and languages
> should serve him.
> His dominion is an everlasting dominion
> that shall not pass away,
> and his kingship is one
> that shall never be destroyed.

John combines this vision of Daniel's with Ps 110:1, "The Lord says to my lord, 'sit at my right hand until I make your enemies your footstool.'" The latter Scripture in particular was an immensely important verse for the early Christians as they interpreted the events of the life, death and resurrection of Jesus (cf. Mark 14:62, Luke 22:69). John closes the sequence of visions of victory with an allusion to Joel:

> Put in the sickle,
> for the harvest is ripe.
> Go in, tread,
> for the wine press is full.
> The vats overflow,
> for their wickedness is great.
> Multitudes, multitudes,
> in the valley of decision!
> For the day of the Lord is near
> in the valley of decision!
> The sun and the moon are darkened,
> and the stars withdraw their shining (Joel 3:13–15).

While John uses this passage as an image of the destruction of the wicked, I believe we are better off seeing this as an image of the destruction of wick*ness*. When Paul wrote "I am convinced that neither death, nor life, nor angels, nor rulers, nor things present, nor things to come, nor powers, nor height, nor depth, nor anything else in all creation, will be able to separate us from the love of God in Christ Jesus our Lord" (Rom 8:38–39), he was saying something similar. Evil will not have the final word in God's plan. One way to affirm that is to speak of the defeat and destruction of those who are perpetrators of evil. But perhaps, in the twenty-first century, living as we do with a more complex understanding of the human psyche, of complex factors in global politics, and generally of the complexity of sin, we might put it another way: reaping with a sickle destroys all evil from the presence of God's eternity, in preparation for the City of God that John will finally see in Rev 21:1.

PORTENTS AND DISCERNMENT—A DIGRESSION ON READING

John's attention is turned back to the heavens, where a new, third portent (following Rev 12:1 and 12:3) is revealed (Rev 15:1). The sequence that begins will wrap up not only human but cosmic history, and at Rev 17:1 we will be entering a chronologically indescribable twilight zone, the moment of God's judgment, the ultimate caesura between that which is familiar and that which is yet to come, that for which all creation yearns (Rom 8:18–25). This is the moment, or passage, or aeon (because in God's eternity there can be no measurement of time: 2 Pet 3:8) that makes sense of all existence, all suffering, and even all joy. The "yes" has been foreshadowed from as long ago as Rev 1:7, where it is often weakly translated "even so" or "so it is to be" in English. For contemporary readers, imagine instead the expression of delight "Yes!" with fist pulled downward. But before the eschatological "yes" of God can be voiced (Rev 16:7, 2 Cor 1:20), before meaning can be found, before perfection, God's "no" must reverberate through fallen creation. There can be no eternal "yes" without God's "no" to evil, suffering, and sin.

It has been said, often attributed to Karl Barth,[27] that Christian people should observe the world with one eye on the Scriptures and the other on the newspaper—today we might say news media in all its forms. However, the media through which we must read the signs of the times can be highly biased and manipulative forces in society, and they can never be unbiased. Media commentators must serve their masters, and whether their masters are governments controlling purse strings or shareholders seeking to nurture a social environment serving the interests of their profits, neutrality is all but unattainable.

Portents: one eye on the Scriptures, and another on news media? Where would we look for a portent today? Rudolf Otto cut to the quick of the matter:

> Whatever has loomed upon the world of his ordinary concerns as something terrifying and baffling to the intellect; whatever among natural occurrences or events in the human, animal or vegetable kingdoms has set him astare in wonder and astonishment—such things have ever aroused in man, and become endued with, the "daemonic dread" and numinous feeling, so as to become "portents," "prodigies," and "marvel."[28]

---

27. Attributed, although no direct quotation is available.
28. Otto, *Holy*, 64.

Shock and Awe (Revelation 10:1–14:20)

But the potential for discernment of the portentous is easily cauterized, either by ourselves or by external circumstances—or, in reality, by both.

In nations where the state has genuinely controlled the media, as Vladimir Putin recently attempted to do with mixed success in the lead up to Russian elections, and as the state-controlled North Korean media ensured they did following the death of Kim Jong-il, government decisions are not open to scrutiny at all. This is true of the dictatorships of right or left: the wings of politics unite in evil. In a nation with few or no state-owned media enterprises, market forces tend to ensure that the wealthiest media enterprises devour all opposition, and themselves become unassailable perpetrators of their own selective truths (as Neil Postman suggested long ago in his book *Amusing Ourselves to Death*[29]). There may though be some, if not many, checks and balances, as ongoing repercussions of the *News of the World* debacle indicate. It is not easy attempting to be a Christian scanning the metaphorical heavens for portents in our current world.

In a post-enlightenment world we are more likely to see portents on a smartphone than in the heavens. In fact, as a thoroughly rationalistic, post-Enlightenment people, Westerners are rarely likely to observe the heavens at all. This can be literally true: visitors to the Cosmos Centre in Charleville in south-west Queensland, where I lived for a while, were often staggered by the number of stars they could see with the naked eye in the night skies. City lights and smog obliterate the skies, but it is not only the lights and smog that obliterate the skies, and the skies are not all that are obliterated. I was on a tram in inner-city Melbourne when on February 8, 1983 a massive dust storm swept down from the Mallee region of Victoria. It all seemed quite normal to me: I had moved to Australia expecting it to be a place of dust storms and fierce heat (it had not occurred to me that Melburnians live in a city south of the majority of the population of my native New Zealand). So I was wrong to consider a Melbourne dust storm to be normality. On the other hand, most other passengers on that Carlton tram were experiencing near-apocalyptic terror: unmitigated city dwellers, they were quarantined from nature, had never before seen a dust storm (nor had I, though later I would find them commonplace in Charleville), and were genuinely, if only briefly, frightened (I was not). There were shrieks and tears in the minutes that followed. This was nature in dramatic mode: to an extent it *was* a portent, for the storm was a direct result of topsoil erosion in northern Victoria and eastern South Australia, and there were lessons to be

---

29. Neil Postman, *Amusing Ourselves*.

learned. Eight days later Victoria, South Australia, and portions of Western Australia and New South Wales were devastated by the Ash Wednesday bush fires. Many of the lives that were lost that day could have been saved if human beings had not allowed themselves to become so blasé about the forces of nature, about the ability of eucalyptus forests to become massive incendiary devices, destroying all in their path.

It is dangerous thing to lose touch with nature. When I was working for the ABC, many of my colleagues were thoroughly and utterly urbanized—*inner*-urbanized, even. Few could understand my obsession with interminable outback and interstate drives, my love of the vastness of inland Australia. I was often asked about the emptiness of the outback, something I have never experienced: "But there's *nothing* there," they protested. It is never empty, it is always changing. It is never even silent, at least in the sense of total absence of sound: always an insect, an animal, or a bird is stirring. It is always, to me, electrifying: "The world is charged with the grandeur of God," wrote Gerard Manley Hopkins. Nature is a portent of the magnificence of the Creator. In the surrounds of unspoiled nature I am reminded of my vulnerability and my insignificance. In the surrounds of unspoiled nature I am reminded of my need for a God who will transcend my vulnerability and my insignificance. "Look at all the stars! The universe just goes out forever and ever," says Calvin (not the theologian!). The sage Hobbes replies, "It kind of makes you wonder why man considers himself such a big screaming deal." But if Calvin is having an epiphanous moment it is soon shattered: "That's why we stay inside with our appliances," he retorts, surrounded by the paraphernalia of an electronic-age living room.[30]

Once, when generating a religious radio documentary on "the bush change phenomenon" (the successor to the sea-change phenomenon once real estate prices had made the latter impossible), I asked Anglican bishop Bruce Wilson, he of the meteorite showers, about the conceptual love of the harshness of the outback that drives some, like me, to escape the city. "Is it the harshness, or is it the vastness?" he mused in reply. Out there, in the vastness, there is a chance to see, hear, and feel the voice of the heavens, the voice of God. Out there, there is a chance to experience God in ways that were well known to the ancients, our John included, but are sadly foreign to those of us trapped in the endless, smog-bound search for survival, if not profit.

---

30. Watterson, *Magical World*, 21.

Shock and Awe (Revelation 10:1–14:20)

I have been privileged in my travels to scratch the surface of the magnificence of a world charged with the grandeur of God. However, the ancients, and those contemporary ancients such as our remote-dwelling Aboriginal sisters and brothers, knew and know well the power of portent. So do some today who take the challenge of escaping the norms of existence. In some Christian communities this may be reflected in an introverted form of prayer life, sometimes referred to as "hesychastic," from the Greek for stillness (the Taizé Community is perhaps the best-known form outside traditional Eastern Orthodox prayer cycles). Proponents of such a prayer life find strength in Matt 6:6: "whenever you pray, go into your room and shut the door and pray to your Father who is in secret." Behaviorally this is the antithesis of a neon-lit world of self-importance.

But this experience is not always liturgical. In her solo journey around the world, then teenage sailor Jessica Watson found time for introspection:

> Watching an amazing sunset, or sunrise, was one of the things that could lift my spirits, especially after a few gloomy days. The different colours that move across the sky as the sun sets, the pinks, blues, inky indigos and purples could be absolutely breathtaking. But whenever I saw a red sky at night I couldn't help but recite to myself the old sailors' saying:

Red sky at night, sailor's delight; Red sky in the morning, sailor's warning.

> Even if Bob [McDavitt, New Zealand Meteorological Ambassador]'s forecast was totally different it always planted the thought in my mind that the color of the sky could predict what was coming. Where does that saying even come from? I had a bit of a search on the internet and it was fascinating to see it goes back to biblical times. They didn't have people like Bob giving them weather forecasts then, so sailors—and shepherds (which is the other version you hear of the rhyme)—had learnt by noting the changes around them, things like the colors of the sky or the direction of the wind, and memorizing the weather that seemed to follow on. Makes sense to me.[31]

Watson, radically outside the strictures of urban existence on her gutsy teenaged journey, processed the power of portent at least to the level that Jesus expected of every intelligent human being (Matt 16:1–4, Luke 12:54–55). In doing so she pushed beyond the normal world-awareness of most Australians, dwellers in what is often considered one of the most urbanized

---

31. Watson, *True Spirit*, 179–80.

nations on earth. The Australian Department of Foreign Affairs and Trade website states, incorrectly as it happens, that "Australia is one of the most urbanized and coast-dwelling populations in the world." In fact, Australia is pushed well outside the top ten urbanized nations by single-city nations such as Monaco, Singapore and the Vatican, and icy realms such as Iceland and Greenland. The case remains: in my adopted country we cling to the coastline, and to our urban jungles. New Zealanders less so, but nevertheless a vast proportion of that country's population dwell in what poet James K. Baxter called (amongst other things) the "megalopolis," the vast sprawling city that is Auckland.

Apocalyptic writers expect at the very least the degree of connection to God's world that Jessica Watson demonstrated. They demand more than that, though. They demand that we can read the timeless signs of human story, too:

> What did you go out into the wilderness to look at? A reed shaken by the wind? What then did you go out to see? Someone dressed in soft robes? Look, those who wear soft robes are in royal palaces. What then did you go out to see? A prophet? Yes, I tell you, and more than a prophet. This is the one about whom it is written,
>
> "See, I am sending my messenger ahead of you, who will prepare your way before you."
>
> Truly I tell you, among those born of women no one has arisen greater than John the Baptist; yet the least in the kingdom of heaven is greater than he (Matt 11:7–11).

If we do not attune ourselves to a state in which God can convey presence, divine meaning and purpose to us in nature and in the human story, then we desensitize ourselves, lamely reaching the point at which portents are gobbledygook, and the voice of God is silenced in our experience.

John sees "another sign in heaven" because he is attuned to the possibilities of God ("I was in the spirit on the Lord's day"—Rev 1:10) in nature and in the human story. Even though he describes what he sees as "great and amazing," it is no more so than the visions that have preceded it. The third great portent, after the seals and the trumpets, is the series of plagues, the final expression of the wrath of God. John uses a different word to most New Testament writers when speaking of God's wrath, but the implication is the same: God is in control, and all that has been seeking to undermine that control must be destroyed for God to be "all in all",[32] or for the work

---

32. As Paul puts it at 1 Cor 15:28, cf. Eph 4:6, Col 3:11.

Shock and Awe (Revelation 10:1–14:20)

of God to be "finished" (Rev 16:17. John uses a different word here, too: *gegōnen*, not the *tetelestai* of John 19:30; our John will often choose a different word to convey the same idea as his namesake).

TURN OR BURN?

John's understanding at this point is that those who are (to borrow Paul's phrase), "in Christ" are inoculated from the divine wrath that follows. His allusion is to Isaiah's apocalyptic vision, with its invitation for the people of God to escape the events unfolding:

> Come, my people, enter your chambers,
> and shut your doors behind you;
> hide yourselves for a little while
> until the wrath is past.
> For the LORD comes out from his place
> to punish the inhabitants of the earth for their iniquity;
> the earth will disclose the blood shed on it,
> and will no longer cover its slain (Isa 26:20–21).

A similar motif underscores the apocalyptic expectations of 1 Thess, both at 1 Thess 1:9b–10 ("you turned to God from idols, to serve a living and true God, and to wait for his Son from heaven, whom he raised from the dead—Jesus, who rescues us from the wrath that is coming") and at 1 Thess 5:9–10 ("God has destined us not for wrath but for obtaining salvation through our Lord Jesus Christ, who died for us, so that whether we are awake or asleep we may live with him"). First Thessalonians was the first of Paul's letters to be written, and it is arguably the most apocalyptic of his letters, providing useful parallels to John's vision.

There is no sense in any of these texts of a voyeuristic delight in the punishment of the wicked, though this can creep through occasionally in the Judeo-Christian tradition, and may underlie Rev 14:10. It is, in the face of persecution, understandable if not attractive psychology, but outside times of persecution it is probably beholden on the Christian community to seek restorative rather than retributive structures of justice. It helps our focus if we remember once again that "wickedness" rather than "the wicked" is the primary focus of God's conclusive intervention. As long ago as 1965, biblical scholar C. F. D. Moule was suggesting that the word "punishment" and other words related to it (especially "retribution") have no legitimate place in Christian thought and practice.³³ Some forms of evangelicalism have held tenaciously to a retributive view, and the hurling of texts and counter texts is unhelpful (as ever). It is sufficient to say at this point that it very hard to imagine an eternal pleasure gained from viewing tortured souls though the glass floor (Rev 4:6, 15:2) of heaven.

James Joyce captures the ambivalence of hellfire theology in *A Portrait of the Artist as a Young Man*.³⁴ He bases his portrayal of hellfire preaching on historical abuses of the book of Revelation—using as inspiration sermons from a seventeenth-century Jesuit preacher, Giovanni Pietro Pinamonti, although the style was by no means peculiar to that tradition or period. The preacher dwells mercilessly on descriptions of hell in order to convert his audience, before depicting the moment of eternal separation:

> Friend is torn apart from friend, children are torn from their parents, husbands from their wives. The poor sinner holds out his arms to those who were dear to him in this earthly world, to those whose simple piety perhaps he made a mock of, to those who counseled him and tried to lead him on the right path, to a kind brother, to a loving sister, to the mother and father who loved him so dearly. But it is too late: the just turn away from the wretched damned souls which now appear before the eyes of all in their hideous and evil character. O you hypocrites, O, you whited sepulchers, O you who present a smooth smiling face to the world while your soul within is a foul swamp of sin, how will it fare with you in that terrible day?³⁵

The celestial liturgy that celebrates the "righteous ordinances" of God celebrates the punishment of the unjust:

> Great and amazing are your deeds,
> Lord God the Almighty!
> Just and true are your ways,
> King of the nations!
> Lord, who will not fear
> and glorify your name?
> For you alone are holy.
> All nations will come
> and worship before you,

---

33. See C. F. D. Moule, "Punishment and Retribution: an Attempt to Delimit their Scope in New Testament Thought", 19. Cited in Marshall, *Beyond Retribution*, 116.

34. There are several editions. I use the reprint edition by Grafton Books, 1977.

35. From chapter 3 in Joyce, *Portrait*, 105.

for your judgments have been revealed (Rev 15:3–4).

At the heart of John's new vision in chapters 15 and 16 is another series of liturgical actions. These include hymn-singing (Rev 15:3–4) and the pouring of what might be termed counter-libations (Rev 16:1–20). The word "liturgy" means "service," appearing first in the Scriptures in Exod 28:35. Paul uses the word in Phil 2:17 and 2:30, though it is often lost in translation; it appears also in Luke 1:23, Heb 8:6, and 9:21. Always underlying the word "liturgy" is a sense of cultic ritual. In our contemporary world, with the notable exception of the Returned and Services League/ Returned Services' Association rites of Australia and New Zealand (and similar returned service personnel rites in other countries), and the fiercely secular and often shapeless rites of citizenship and civic award ceremonies (including the bestowal of academic degrees), the action and shapeliness of liturgy is largely lost.

Liturgy is therefore a strongly countercultural activity, even, in Brueggemann's terms, prophetic. It provides, in the materialistic terms that are the mainstay of our social fabric, no *practical* purpose (except the manufacture and purchase of "consumables," products necessary to carry out the rites themselves). In the ancient world it was countercultural in a slightly different sense: liturgy itself was common to almost every religious subculture, and it was a part of the self-definition and boundary maintenance of those cultures. Libations had to be poured out (an image picked up several times by John), offerings had to be made, incense and candles burned to appease the gods—including the emperor. It was possible to take part in various religious subcultures, but Christianity drew an impenetrable boundary: God or God-in-Christ alone was worthy of worship (Rev 19:10–11). A political and religious line was drawn in the sand, and John like many other Christ-followers demanded that the Christian community did not traverse that line. Not much has changed: in the materialistically unproductive actions of liturgy, the Christian community states that materialism (most obscenely conspicuous at Christmas) is not its highest value.

Often, though, the celebration of that which is valued will entail a shadow side, sometimes but not always unspoken. As citizenship certificates are handed out at civil ceremonies, there will be no thought or word spoken about those who are refugees from war or famine or both, or for example, those who have died on the Arafura or Timor Seas, desperately seeking to start a newer, safer life but unable for whatever reason to follow appropriate procedure. Nor will there be thought of those who made it across the sea but who descend into hellholes of depression and self-abuse behind the razor wire of detention centers, popular footballs of political ideology. These hellholes are mainly hidden from public scrutiny, either on the mainland of Australia or in the remote locations cruelly designated the "Pacific Solution" or "Malaysian Solution," depending on the political party administering boundary maintenance. "Pacific Solution" or "Malaysian Solution": these titles resonate with obscene echoes of another regime's "final solution." There will be no thought at a civic liturgy of citizenship of those who await "processing," a verb that macabrely mimics the processing of animals at a slaughterhouse and ignores an inconvenient truth that these are human beings attempting to start new lives free from bombs and landmines.

John's vision of a celestial liturgy is not immune from a shadow side. Human psychology permeates the language of faith. In a paper presented a decade ago, I described a parallel example: Daniel Defoe, if read naively, can appear to be a highly individualistic opportunist reveling in the destruction of native communities and habitats. In a post-colonial reading of his works, such as one undertaken by Bernard McGrane in his *Beyond Anthropology*, Defoe can wrongly be seen as a perpetrator of exploitation and cultural annihilation.[36] So, too, it is *de rigueur* today to see much missionary endeavor of the nineteenth century in terms of exploitative darkness. While some missionaries were standing between hunters' guns and their intended Yolŋu victims, others were aiding the exploitation of Indigenous peoples.

While Defoe—or our John—can be interpreted to be dancing on the graves of those who have been defeated, as McGrane's approach to Defoe suggests, this interpretation ignores the authors' and visionaries' original place in history. Defoe constantly celebrated his heroes' financial gain, a fact McGrane deplores as an example of individualized and capitalist greed. But context, as I have said, is everything: Defoe was writing not as a powerful oppressor, but as an oppressed non-conformist or Dissenter, to whom economic growth was the only counterbalance to Anglican mastery of the corridors of power. As I have said elsewhere,

> Defoe's economic opportunism must be seen not through the eyes of late twentieth century environmental, ethnic and economic correctness, which is McGrane's error. Instead Defoe was, in historical context, dreaming the powerfully subversive dream of power for the powerless, a dream of justice for the Dissenters who were

---

36. Godfrey, "Defoe's Ego."

Shock and Awe (Revelation 10:1–14:20)

disenfranchised at every opportunity by the dominant, Erastian[37] Anglican machine.[38]

John was, while seemingly dancing on the graves of the victims of God's wrath, in reality doing no more than expressing the relief of an oppressed person who finally sees his persecutor fall. Even a canonical vision can be permeated with the humanity of the visionary, for, as I noted in my opening chapter, a biblical author was not engaging in some uncanny form of "automatic writing," transcribing the infallible words of a celestial dictator.

In the imagery of Rev 15, John draws together what Aune calls "a pastiche of lyrical fragments,"[39] combining Old Testament texts to represent the songs of heaven. For the Jewish people, celebration of the saving acts of God made those acts present once again (just as in many rites of Australian Aboriginal cultures the ancient events of the Dreamtime are made present once again). By celebrating these acts in his heavenly vision of the end of time, John traces God's footprints throughout and beyond human history, singing songs of deliverance in the style of Moses and the escapees from Egypt. The song John records can be compared with Exod 15:1–18 or Deut 31:30—32:43, great songs of deliverance that for John foreshadow God's final and eternal deliverance of his people from suffering.

The song of Revelation 15 foretells all nations coming to worship God. History, while as yet incomplete, suggests a degree of unfulfilled optimism in the expectation: at no stage in human history has the God of Jesus Christ been universally worshipped. Nevertheless, it was a hope that became increasingly central to the late centuries of the Old Testament era, as the Hebrew prophets began to foretell Israel's role as a beacon to the world.[40] It is a hope to which the Christian people of God may still hold fast. We have no right to condemn the nations—our history is far too shoddy for that—but in our own liturgical acts of intercession we must hold all the varieties of peoples in the healing light of Christ. We will, of course, name before God nations suffering calamity (at time of writing I continue to think of and pray for the people of Yemen, Syria and Afghanistan, Somalia, Ethiopia, North and South Sudan, and West

---

37. Thomas Erastus, 1524–1583, is generally if somewhat incorrectly understood to be the architect of a theology by which the church is largely subservient to the state. I use his name in that sense to describe aspects of state-church relationship that undergird seventeenth-century Anglican liturgy and theology.

38. Godfrey, "Defoe's Ego," 88.

39. Aune, *Revelation 6–16*, 874.

40. See Isa 2:2–4, 14:1–2, 45:14, 60:1–3, 66:18, Jer 16:19, Zech 8:20–23.

Papua, to name just some in times of political turmoil or oppression), but we need to hold before God all peoples, for all peoples bear the indelible image of God. We may pray in purely evangelistic terms for the opening of borders to credible Christian witness (we might think of North Korea, in particular, or the more militant Islamic nations), but we might pray also in the hope that one day all peoples learn to live justly, sharing the resources of the earth, eradicating the brutal divide between what we now call the "global north," the rich nations, and the "global south." It is my own belief that divide will never disappear on this side of the *eschaton* that John describes, yet we must never cease to pray and work for it, practicing, effectively, the eternities of God. By praying and working for justice we join Paul in the great apocalyptic prayer of 1 Cor 16:22: *Maranatha*.

In the song that John hears, he hears a celebration of the unveiling of the righteous judgments, the "right ordinances" of God. In context it *is* a celebration of God's punishment of the wicked, but I will always maintain, as I have said above, that it is a celebration of the destruction of wickedness. Christians surrender at great cost a sense of the holiness and righteousness of God, and any theology that downplays the seriousness of sin is an insult to the self-sacrificial life and witness of Christ. Throughout Revelation there are hints that God's standards of salvation are not limited to our expectations, our theology, or our sacraments. But in John's vision are the legions of heaven dancing on the graves of those that are excluded from God's presence, the inhabitants of hell?

Evangelist and apologist Rob Bell has incurred the wrath of fellow evangelicals by addressing this question, albeit primarily with reference to non-believers rather than anti-believers. His conclusion, that the notion of a once loving, inviting cosmic creator who suddenly at the moment of a non-believer's death turns into a "a cruel, mean, vicious tormenter"[41] is something of a doctrinal obscenity has upset those for whom eternal punishment is a fundamental doctrine of faith.

Some interpreters of the "righteous ordinances" of God see the eternal punishment of such people to be implied by texts such as Revelation, and indeed there is in some circles an apoplectic response to anything suggested that appears to blur the boundaries of salvation (Albert Mohler, president of the Southern Baptist Theological Seminary and a leading conservative evangelical in the US, described Bell's book *Love Wins* as "theologically disastrous"[42]). Sometimes the credibility gap between our experience of

---

41. Bell, *Love Wins*, 173–174.
42. Meacham, "Pastor Rob," 1.

the love of loved ones and a doctrine of eternal punishment for those of them who reject our faith has been overcome by suggesting that, once the veneers and deceptions of civilization are removed in the eschatological judgment, the vileness of those we have presumed to love will repulse us for all eternity. This chilling theological (technically "soteriological") contortion is caricatured by James Joyce in the closure of the sermon cited earlier. Earlier, in his preacher-persona, Joyce depicted a moment when "Every sin would then come forth from its lurking place, the most rebellious against the divine will and the most degrading to our poor corrupt nature, the tiniest imperfection and the most heinous atrocity."[43] Joyce depicts a moment at which God turns from beckoning welcomer to draconian executioner, the moment Bell refuses to conceive of: "The particular judgment was over and the soul had passed to the abode of bliss or to the prison of purgatory or had been hurled howling into hell."[44]

In the Joycean vision of judgment, the events depicted work their wonders on a tender soul, but not as the preacher intended. Dedalus, Joyce's central (and partially auto-biographical) character, is first persuaded by the apocalyptic terrors of the sermon, but is then repulsed by this hellfire and brimstone rhetoric. Dedalus, like Joyce his creator, leaves this kind of judgment scene and any semblance of orthodox Christianity behind him. He can hardly be blamed for it. It is not a scene that fills the reader with confidence at the joys of heaven: "Can a woman forget her nursing child, or show no compassion for the child of her womb?" asks Isaiah (Isa 49:15). As the "saved" mother strides confidently into heaven's eternity (with its glassy floors through which to view the damned in torment), will she gleefully sing the songs of God while her child cowers at the gateway of an eternal hell? It is a question I believe we must put to the scenes of apocalyptic. Patrick White left church fellowship when he found Christians to be so mean-minded that they rejected as evil guessing games at a fair. Joyce, like White, turned away to seek meaning elsewhere. Have the evangelists like those depicted by Joyce, or the bean-averse rector of Patrick White's experience, evangelized? Or has theirs been an obscene parody of evangelism? And having rejected an obscene parody of evangelism, must the reprobates burn eternally in hell while "the chosen" dance on the glass ceiling of their fiery graves?

43. Joyce, *Portrait*, 104.
44. Ibid.

Babylon's Cap

Rob Bell suggests an alternative hermeneutic (interpretational method) when faced by Scriptures that present scenes and judgment of separation: "may you know, deep in your bones, that love wins."[45] Frederic Farrar, who was Dean of Westminster, put the underlying issue neatly in an 1877 sermon in Westminster Abbey: "how long, even after death, man may continue to resist [God's] will; how long he may continue in that spiritual death which is alienation from God; that is one of the secret things which God hath not revealed."[46] It may be that it is this victory of divine love over human weakness that undergirds John's vision of judgment, and that we can therefore, for our loved ones, find a word of hope in the "righteous ordinances" celebrated in the eternal song John hears sung in the heavens.

If that is the case, there may well be in the heavenly liturgy a celebration of hope for all those who we love. Yet at the same time we cannot deny that history is littered with great evil, not the kind of manufactured evil that James Joyce foists on his central character. Am I assuming that, when we are with John's celestial choir celebrating God's righteous judgments, God merely waves a magic wand, setting to rights the immeasurable atrocities of an Adolf Hitler, Joseph Stalin, Pol Pot, Radovan Karadžić, Ratko Mladić, serial killer Ivan Milat, or a serial sexual predator (perhaps one who practiced their evil within the faith community)? Is a gunman such as New Zealand town Aramoana's David Gray or Australian town Port Arthur's Martin Bryant or Norway's Anders Breivik to be seen as in some way more forgivable because they killed fewer people than Hitler or Stalin? What of the upright and moral Australian police who hunted and killed Aboriginal men, women and children in the Forrest River (or Oombulgurri) region of northern Australia in 1926 (records vary widely from thirteen to three hundred or more victims)? What of the leadership of the Anglican Church, who turned a blind eye to the plight of West Australian Aboriginal people and ignored the missionary John Gribble who sought to protect and speak out for them—including the Oombulgurri victims—and left him a broken and desolate man, prematurely dead at 43?[47] If some missionaries had liter-

---

45. Bell, *Love Wins*, 197–98.

46. Farrar, *Eternal Hope*, 86.

47. For the story of John Brown Gribble see Harris, *One Blood*, 407–27. For Gribble's role in the Oombulgurri context see his report to the "Royal Commission into the Killing and Burning of Bodies of Aborigines in East Kimberley, and into Police Methods when Effecting Arrest," vol. 1 of *West Australian Proceedings of Parliament and Papers*, 1928 (in S. Stone, ed., *Aborigines in White Australia: A Documentary History of the Attitudes Affecting Official Policy and Australian Aborigines 1967–1973*. Melbourne: Heinemann,

ally stood in front of the guns of those hunting Aboriginal people, Gribble did so metaphorically. Evil has many faces—and, for that matter, what evil might you or I perpetrate by action or passive inaction if the circumstances were right (or, indeed, horribly wrong)?

A theology of universal salvation must ensure it is not proposing that God simply pats perpetrators of terror on the back and tells them "never mind, don't do it again, eternally." Perhaps, and to be honest, we must all remain slightly agnostic on this question. There is a point at which a human being has, by their life choices, obliterated their own vestiges of humanity. Chris Marshall refers to a doctrine of final judgment, which he describes as "unique and truly definitive," and as such truly exceptional:

> In all other situations where offenders are dealt with, an appeal can be made to some remaining goodness within them, however residual, to promote restoration. By contrast, anyone who is destroyed at the eschatological judgment will have become so totally identified with all that is evil that nothing remains of their personality to be restored.[48]

Although he is portraying a more archetypally traditional judgment scene—and utilizing the narratives of Islam as much as Christianity—the Gothic novelist William Beckford captured such an annihilative possibility at the end of his dark novella *Vathek*. As one of the perpetrators of evil at last encounters divine justice,

> a voice, proceeding from the abyss of death, proclaimed, "All is accomplished!" Instantaneously the haughty forehead of the intrepid princess became corrugated with agony; she uttered a tremendous yell, and fixed, no more to be withdrawn, her right hand upon her heart, which was become a receptacle of eternal fire.[49]

Beckford, although partially utilizing an Islamic world view, deliberately alludes to the "it is done" of Rev 21:6. Unlike Marshall, Beckford is still imagining a final retributive judgment, in which those who have been the most unmitigated perpetrators of evil are trapped in an eternal torment.

Charles Dickens, by no means a theologian nor even greatly inclined to Christian orthodoxy, offers a more salient literary example of

---

1974). Cited in Behrendt, "Genocide," 145.

48. Marshall, *Beyond Retribution*, 195.

49. Beckford, "Vathek," 253–54.

annihilative judgment when the evil Mr. Krook spontaneously combusts midway through *Bleak House*:

> Call the death by any name Your Highness will, how you will, attribute it to whom you will, or say it might have been prevented how you will, it is the same death eternally—inborn, inbred, engendered in the corrupted humors of the vicious body itself, and that only—Spontaneous Combustion, and none other of all the deaths that can be died.[50]

Dickens is not endeavoring to depict an eschatological judgment, but his may be a more useful depiction of eschatological annihilation of a being so utterly consumed by evil that they have desiccated every shred of humanity within themselves as it were "beyond redemption." Marshall though is careful to ensure that even if such an eternally annihilative alternative exists, it is not cheapened as Christians have so often cheapened it, not used as a threat to coerce all who do not match the image of the saved (as envisaged by the Christians), as it often has been when Christianity has become not the voice of the oppressed but of the oppressive dominant culture:

> The utter uniqueness of this situation precludes using it to avoid a commitment to restoration in every other situation we face; if God works for restoration up until the very last moment, so must we. It also precludes using the last Judgment as a justification or paradigm for corresponding human action in present history, as happened during the Inquisition, for example. To the contrary, God's prerogative of final judgment challenges and critiques—rather than validates and underwrites—violent human retribution on wrongdoers (Rom 12:19–21). "God is not needed to create guilt or to punish," Albert Camus once said. "Our fellow-men suffice, aided by ourselves. You were speaking of the last Judgment. Allow me to laugh respectfully. I shall wait for it resolutely, for I have known what is worse, the judgment of men."[51]

This is the question we must hold in tension with its counterbalance: are perpetrators of evil beyond the reach of grace? Is their evil, rather than God's grace, the final word reverberating throughout eternity? Somewhere the answer dwells in stories of the tough love that God dispenses to his Hebrew people throughout their Scriptures. Many times the people are

---

50. Dickens, *Bleak House*, 36.
51. Marshall, *Beyond Retribution*, 195. Marshall cites Camus, *The Fall*, 110 (81 in his edition).

punished for their perpetrations of evil, and many times God corrects them, welcoming them home. Perhaps the love of God is so great that the dance of heaven is withheld until the last reprobate finally sees the enormity of their sin, the gap between their evil and the holiness of Christ, and like an alcoholic at an AA meeting, finally surrenders to the Christ who beckons. I must be careful: I live a privileged armchair existence, and have never been on the wrong end of the sheer evil of a serial killer in the Belanglo Forest of New South Wales, nor watched in terror the manic rampage of Norwegian serial killer Anders Behring Breivik, nor experienced the depraved atrocities perpetrated by a Charles Manson. But even in such cases, might not God's capacity to redeem extend further than human capacities for evil?

5

It Is Done! (Revelation 15:1—20:15)

THESE HAVE BEEN LONG digressions, but necessary ones, because John's vision has reached now to the end of time. We return to his vision to find angels carrying out liturgical acts, pouring out God's judgments across the face of the universe. One by one, bowls carrying atrocities that are directly reminiscent, but in magnified form, of the plagues of Egypt are emptied on the earth. Are God's judgments punitive or redemptive? Sores, corpses, blood, heat, darkness, and fiendish creatures are all poured out. Then, in words reminiscent of those used by Jesus on the cross, "it is done," the liturgical and punitive actions cease: "the cities of the nations fell" (Rev 16:19), and the islands and mountains fled. Yet it is not quite done, for the crescendo of this phase of punishment is the arrival of fifty-kilogram hailstorms. The scenes and their punishments were never meant to be seen consecutively: these are accumulative images of the dark side of God's wrath. There has been throughout this outpouring of wrath an allusion to Jer 7:20: "Therefore thus says the Lord GOD: My anger and my wrath shall be poured out on this place, on human beings and animals, on the trees of the field and the fruit of the ground; it will burn and not be quenched". God is not a playmate, and Rudolf Otto rightly reminds us that the fearful nature of God, God's wrath, is a central scriptural theme.[1] Aslan is not a tame lion.

This time there is no caesura before the final action, and the scene moves quickly to introduce the formidable but doomed figure of the "the great whore" (also at Rev 19:2; just "whore" at Rev 17: 5, 15 and 16). This eschatological figure reinforces the feminist critique that women in the

1. Otto, *Holy*, 18.

It Is Done! (Revelation 15:1—20:15)

Judeo-Christian scriptural traditions are often typecast as either sexual temptress (Eve) or sexless servant (Mary); there is much truth in that delineation. Our Scriptures are a product of their societies of origin, and there have been improvements in the world we live and serve God in. Some in theological circles are optimistic in terms of human evolution towards perfection; Pierre Teilhard de Chardin and the process theologians, for example, see humankind and its behavior on a relentless march towards the perfected reign of God, the Omega Point, as Teilhard calls it. I am not so optimistic in terms of human progress, but do accept that there have been eddies of progress in history, and waves of feminist "conscientization" have in the last one hundred and fifty years have made us increasingly aware of our cultural misogyny. We can to some extent "de-genderize" the whore figure of John's writing, so that it becomes all that seduces the world's political and economic leaders from paths of compassion and justice. The Eve-whore is counterbalanced by another feminine image in the book of Revelation, the chaste Marian image of the heavenly woman clothed with the sun (chapter 12); ultimately we must accept that John used the visionary material available to him faithfully and to the best of his ability. As feminist biblical theologian Elizabeth Schüssler Fiorenza put it, "The female imagery of Revelation . . . would be completely misconstrued if it were understood as referring to the actual behavior of individual women."[2]

Whoredom is a recurrent image of evil in the Hebrew Scriptures,[3] the term appearing some fifty-eight times in forty-six verses. Jeremiah, Ezekiel, and Hosea are the main users of the image, and for the Hebrews their terminology resonated with a deep fear of inappropriate sexual behavior which compromises the call to serve God in holiness. This ethos was taken over in the New Testament, and probably best theologized by Paul at 1 Cor 6:16: "Do you not know that whoever is united to a prostitute becomes one body with her? For it is said, 'The two shall be one flesh.'" Paul did not, unlike one or two historical cult leaders, envisage this as a form of evangelism!

John uses the image of whoredom as a representation of all that corrupts human leadership, but he is also adopting a well-utilized Hebrew image and deliberately merging it with a favored image of the Roman Empire. The goddess Roma became, once she was incorporated into the imperial cult, the personification of the seat of power. Her pre-Roman cultic origins,

---

2. Fiorenza, *Revelation*, 96.

3. See Isa 1:21, 23:16–17, Nah 3:4, Jer. 3:6–20, Ezek 16:15–22, 23:1–49, Hos 4:12–13, 5:3.

as John may have known, were in the corporate narrative and beliefs of the city of Smyrna, one of the locations to whose churches he is primarily writing. Roma was often depicted as seated, holding the fate of the imperial city in her right hand: John is plunging a lance into the heart of Roman pride, depicting Roman power in terms of prostitution.

As he depicts the impact of the whore on God's world, John is not primarily considering sexual mores and behaviors, but is condemning political opportunism, exploitation, and oppression. The Roman Empire has entered relationships of exploitation and oppression with client-states: at the forefront of John's consciousness is the opportunistic and exploitative relationship that Rome has with Palestine. This relationship was deeply offensive to all those of Hebrew heritage who opposed external authority. Rome is depicted as becoming drunk, not because at this point John is condemning alcohol abuse—though no doubt he like Paul would have little time for that—but because the Roman Empire is sapping the resources and energies of God's "land of milk and honey."

Any community that has been invaded and annexed, and which sees its resources leached away to the benefit of distant peoples can understand John's image. It is an image that dwells at the heart of post-colonial anger as peoples as diverse as Yolŋu, Māori, Inuit or Ibo—again to name just some—see their lands stripped bare, lifestyles decimated, languages annihilated, religious practices shattered, and receive only minimal if any benefit from Europeanization. It is a moment at which the majority of us, as Western- or European-heritage Christians, must ask whether we are standing in solidarity with John's people of God or are ourselves deeply enmeshed in dalliance with Babylon and its whore. Luke Timothy Johnson puts it another way: "Who can deny the sting of the liberationist charge that the church has often represented just those patterns of repression and oppression that reveal not the rule of God but the rule of Satan?"[4] Whose cap are we wearing? We need to be very careful before dancing on the graves of those excluded at the judgment scenes of apocalyptic.

If there is any merit in this form of interpretation, then we must, if we find ourselves at this point separated by our history from John's oppressed people, ask ourselves and ask our text if all is lost. John has dropped enough hints already that this is not the case, but we have historically, and perhaps personally, tended to see ourselves not as in dalliance with the whore but as singing praises with the redeemed. Are we? John's intended audience were,

---

4. Johnson, *Creed*, 259.

but they were a victimized and oppressed people. Again: we must be careful. If the text speaks to us at all about some degree of culpability, then we should remember that the gospel response to guilt is always absolution and redemption. A post-colonial theology of the book of Revelation, should, if it is to remain faithful to the vision of the author, preserve a narrative of individual salvation and continuation after death and after the *eschaton*, rather than a merely political revolution and transformation. Not all contemporary interpreters will accept this; however, to do so is to endure an "other-worldly" dimension that should, at the very least, have us squirming at a place of judgment, the place to which John's vision has now brought us. To do so is to take on our shoulders not only the weight of missed political opportunity, but the greater weight of missed missiological opportunity. Do I waltz into "heaven" singing the songs of the redeemed? After such knowledge, what forgiveness? T. S. Eliot's famous line from "Gerontion" drives to the heart of a vision like John's:

> After such knowledge, what forgiveness? Think now
> History has many cunning passages, contrived corridors
> And issues, deceives with whispering ambitions,
> Guides us by vanities. Think now
> She gives when our attention is distracted
> And what she gives, gives with such supple confusions
> That the giving famishes the craving. Gives too late
> What's not believed in, or if still believed,
> In memory only, reconsidered passion. Gives too soon
> Into weak hands, what's thought can be dispensed with
> Till the refusal propagates a fear. Think
> Neither fear nor courage saves us. Unnatural vices
> Are fathered by our heroism. Virtues
> Are forced upon us by our impudent crimes.
> These tears are shaken from the wrath-bearing tree.[5]

"Neither fear nor courage saves us": the word "grace" does not appear often in the book of Revelation, but it does appear, twice. It appears at the very opening, at Rev 1:4, where John greets the audiences within the seven churches. It appears at the very end, the very last verse, in the familiar phrase "The grace of the Lord Jesus be with all the saints. Amen." The "amen" is God's final word to creation. Neither fear nor courage saves us when we dance with the great whore, but "no" is not the final word of John's vision.

---

5. Eliot, *Collected Poems*, 30.

Nevertheless, care is always needed. For too long, as James Joyce and Patrick White were reminding us, we have seen God's "yes" as neatly embracing us, we have seen ourselves dancing with the redeemed, but have failed to see our flirtations with the whoredom. When reading the final chapters of Revelation, we need to remove from our lenses any sense that we are rightfully joining the victor's song. We must encounter, in Eliot's or even Otto's terms, the wrath of God before we can shed the tears that bring us back to the arms of God.

John in his vision moves to the desert, but this is not the desert of redemptive encounter with God's Spirit. This is far closer to Eliot's wasteland, in turn representing the harsh visions of Ezekiel more familiar to John's audience.[6] In the desert John sees the whore-figure bejeweled, "clothed in purple and scarlet." These are adornments not unknown to the allures of prostitution, but to a Hebrew-influenced audience John may be flagging another contrast. At Acts 16:11–15, Luke recounts an encounter between Paul and Lydia, the latter described as "from the city of Thyatira" and a "dealer in purple cloth" (Luke was probably writing after John, so I am not implying influence here). Purple cloth was made purple by dyeing with the shellfish *murex trunculus* or *murex brandaris*, rendering those involved ritually unclean, according to the Torah (Lev 11:10–12). It is probable that Lydia and the women with her were particularly open to the gospel as they were ritually unclean, on account of their trade, and ostracized by orthodox Jews. They quickly accepted the gospel (Acts 16:14–15): by contrast, the whore of John's vision remains trapped in her purple adornments, immersed in her uncleanness. There is a vivid illustration of the human need for grace in this contrast between Luke's humble gospel-recipient from Thyatira and, in John's vision written in part for the church at Thyatira (and no doubt Philippi), the celestial whore of Babylon. Whether Lydia remained in Philippi or returned to her home town of Thyatira, her story would have been known to John's audience, and the contrast between Lydia's rejection of a purple lifestyle and the whore epitomizing all that purple and scarlet implied was a potent local image.

W. E. H. Stanner warned us in chapter 2, as he alluded to the missionaries' observation of what appeared to be orgiastic practices, that one culture's abominations may be another culture's celebration of life and its cycles. At what point are we traversing the fine line between the letter and the spirit of the law? Defoe wrestled with the question nearly four centuries

---

6. See Ezek 3:12, 14, 8:3, 11:1, 24, 37:1, 43:5.

It Is Done! (Revelation 15:1—20:15)

ago, musing through the persona of Robinson Crusoe as he encountered Indigenous peoples:

> I began with cooler and calmer thoughts to consider what it was I was going to engage in; what authority I had, to pretend to be judge and executioner upon these men as criminals, whom Heaven had thought fit for so many ages to suffer unpunished.[7]

A traditional position, adopted by Defoe, is to see depravity itself as punishment for human failure to acknowledge the God of the Hebrews, and to see "immorality as the punishment not the guilt."[8] It is however doubtful whether, in the context in which I am writing, such an interpretation can be readily applied to local Indigenous communities: Australia's Aboriginal nations existed for some forty or more millennia, by most timelines, before the Hebrews received their Torah, and whatever rites the missionaries cited by Stanner actually saw, the practitioners had not heard the teachings of Moses.

Yet we cannot dismiss the notion of evil with which John is confronting us. Crusoe's decision to intervene in the cannibalism which was about to end the life of another cannibal, whom he subsequently named Friday, is unlikely to be condemned by any contemporary world view, no matter how humanistic. On the other hand, there was also his decision to subjugate Friday by forcing him into European dress, never mind that "wearing the drawers was very awkward to him, and the sleeves of the wastcoat [sic] galled his shoulders and the inside of his arms."[9] A few calluses were, it seems, a small price to pay for the benefits of Europeanization! At this point Crusoe, and probably Defoe, has been generally recognized to be overstepping gospel proclamation values.

Is there a rule by which we can evaluate cultural practices that are alien to the outsider—and in many cases to the conquering or dominating culture? In a remarkable chapter entitled "Oppression and Justice," the outspoken Croatian theologian Miroslav Volf calls to mind the clash of cultures between the British colonial powers, under the leadership of General Charles Napier, and the Brahmans of what is now the Sind Province of India.

> When the British came, one of the colonial impositions they instituted was the prohibition of *sati*—of widows being cremated on their husbands' funeral pyres. They were shrewd enough to

---

7. Defoe, *Robinson Crusoe*, 177.
8. Käsemann, *Romans*, 39; cf. Godfrey, Defoe's Ego," 83.
9. Defoe, *Robinson Crusoe*, 211.

> tolerate a number of native peculiarities, but not the burning of widows. The Brahmans of Sind, however, defended *sati* as an age-old custom. General Napier's response was a simple as it was arrogant: "My nation also has a custom. When men burn women alive, we hang them. Let us all act according to national custom!"[10]

Napier was right. But the Brahmans saw this in another way. To them, "when a husband dies, his wife continues to belong to him and can therefore be cremated on the funeral pyre, presumably feeling no pain because the power of *sat* has descended on her. To offset the damage, she might be worshiped as a goddess."[11] Napier and his Judeo-Christian culture believed in the singular worth of every being as an individual, and that the violation of a life should be met with punitive, and probably retributive, justice. As Volf notes, with hindsight we might criticize the Brahmans for their devaluation of women's individuality, while criticizing Napier for his harshly imposed British retributive justice. We need, though, to be self-critical. As colonialists, Europeans, standing with Defoe in a Judeo-Christian heritage, abhorred cannibalism. But we might learn that, as Volf put it, "our justice might not be as just as we think."[12] We have overseen a destruction of languages and cultures that represents little less than genocide.

There is in our present culture a degree of anger directed at the once-dominant colonial cultures, and at the Christian religion which was intrinsically linked to them. As Volf, among countless others, makes clear, the anger is not unwarranted. To recognize and acknowledge our fault is not a black armband view of history. On the other hand, neither British, nor European, nor Christian history has a copyright on the annihilation of languages: "lest we think it is all about Western imperial powers, over 600 years ago the Incas did it just as effectively, imposing their language, Quechua, on hundreds of tribes on the *altiplano* that they assimilated during the creation of their empire based around Cuzco in present day Peru."[13] The implication of the book of Revelation is that if Babylon's cap fits our collective head, then the onus is on us to be conspicuous in our commitment to Christlike redemptive, ameliorative reaction. Apocalyptic speaks a stern word to us, warning us that as we amalgamate the narratives of history and

---

10. Volf, *Exclusion and Embrace*, 193. Volf is citing in part Peter Berger's *A Far Glory: The Quest for Faith in an Age of Credulity*, New York: Free Press, 1992, 71.

11. Ibid., citing van den Bosch, "Burning Question."

12. Ibid., 195.

13 Davidson, *Planet Word*, 77.

It Is Done! (Revelation 15:1—20:15)

Scripture, we need to do so cautiously. We need to be countercultural and conspicuous by our readiness to turn back to the confessional. The Lamb who "loves us and freed us from our sins by his blood" (Rev 1:5) did not do so by waving a magically redemptive wand over us while we nonchalantly continued our Christ-less journeys. John calls us, when we find in ourselves the traits of the Ephesian, Sardisian or Laodicean churches, to turn again to the confessional, to the healing faith practices of confession, reconciliation, restoration, and perhaps only then absolution. At the heart of John the Seer's theology is judgment: whenever Babylon's cap fits us, then we need the forgiving and redemptive action of the Lamb.

If missionaries are confronted with cultural practices that appear to be an utter abomination to them, then subjugation of such practices and brutal subjection of the practitioners is an all too human response. While in my opinion Barbara Kingsolver's *The Poisonwood Bible* weakens the effectiveness of her much-admired novel by erroneously conflating too many images of colonial missionaries into one missionary stereotype, it is nevertheless this fear of the other, fear of the new and unfamiliar, that she sets about denigrating in the missionary endeavor, epitomized in the cruel figure of Nathan Price. There is fuel enough for Kingsolver's fires: missionaries have made many mistakes out of misunderstandings and fear. But mistakes are not the only dimension to the missionary narrative, and Kingsolver and others might pause to reflect on the missionaries standing in front of the hunters' guns. The hunters had gone many steps further in degradation, coming to see the foreign Aboriginal culture as sub- or non-human. They removed from the Indigenous culture, we could say in a Judeo-Christian tradition, the *imago dei*, the image or mark of God bestowed at creation (Gen 1:27, cf. Rev 7:3). By this the hunters have themselves taken on the counter-mark, the Mark of the Beast (Rev 13:16–18). The hunters have become the timeless whore of John's vision. Humans do this when they descend into the hellish depths of xenophobia. Humans do this when in Burundi and Rwanda Hutus turn on Tutsis and turn rivers into bloodbaths. Humans do this when in Bosnia and Herzegovina Serbs turn on Croats in a frenzy of slaughter. Humans do this when we turn a blind eye to Hitler's thugs in the night, or denigrate the US as the great Satan, or stereotype Muslims as terrorists or gays as faggots. The whore of the vision then is not either gender- or time-specific. She is the epitome of evil and of the seductiveness of sin.

Babylon's Cap

The related notion of the "attractiveness of sin" is an account of all that can seduce the Christ-community from its task of authentic living and proclamation of the values of God, in whatever era it is called to live. John of Patmos is operating out of a heterosexual male psyche and adopting feminine imagery of erotic attraction. It need not be so: "the attractiveness of sin increases through the influx of alluring thoughts and affections, and the power of the will is diminished."[14] The whore can take many forms, not least that of political power. In John's vision she spawns many children, the children of Babylon, which are the cities particularly of the Jewish lands overrun by Roman might, in which cults of the goddess Roma established and flourished.

This whore-goddess sits on the beast, which is now seven mountains, an unsubtle allusion to the seven hills of Rome. The identity of the Beast is revealed to John, and through John to those who respond to his vision, so that they might be protected from uninformed seduction to the demonic and counter-gospel allures of the Roman state. This too is unceasing temptation, for while the democratic states in which most of us are living, and certainly within which I have almost always lived, are not the same as the unchecked power and potential evil of the Roman Empire, they can at times overstep their mark, their limits of propriety, and will need to be called to order by the flawed processes of democracy. Our states too will at times need to be called to order, as best we can call them, when they perpetrate acts and attitudes that are counter to the values of Jesus Christ. The Occupy movement that was, as I first wrote these words, drawing attention to global economic greed will not strike all observers or even participants as a movement proclaiming "reign of God" attitudes, but we might see it something of the face of the Christ who took the bullwhip to the Temple (John 2:15). Pussy Riot's performance in a Moscow church might not strike everyone as a movement proclaiming "reign of God" attitudes, and it certainly did not strike the church leadership as such, but perhaps we might see them, too, as an echo of Jesus and his bullwhip?

Participants do not always remember the cause or their aggression: in the riots following the police shooting of Mark Duggan in London in August 2011, many joined for the bloodlust of the anarchy itself ("things fall apart, the center cannot hold," said Yeats). Yet out of chaos and blood, life can sometimes grow. It may yet be that out of the ugliness of these events, some parties may attempt to redress cycles of violence and destruction, just

---

14. Schade, *Doctrine*, 175.

It Is Done! (Revelation 15:1—20:15)

as, out of the Arab Spring, new and just communities may grow. Always, as Desmond Tutu put it, "if you are neutral in a situation of injustice, you have chosen the side of the oppressor. If an elephant has his foot on the tail of the mouse, and you say you are neutral, the mouse will not appreciate your neutrality."[15]

John was not foretelling mere revolution, because every Robespierre will lead to Directors,[16] and every Hosni Mubarak will make way for the army, with associated risks. Every stumbled human step towards a new and just society might well be considered a foretaste of God's final "no" to evil. Yet there are immeasurable complexities. Was the rioting of some Christians in response to Andres Serrano's 1987 photographic art piece *Piss Christ*,[17] or of some Muslims in response to Danish newspaper *Jyllands-Posten*'s publication of cartoons offensive to Islam, or anger directed by some Muslims at the West in response to a YouTube posting of a weak anti-Islamic film, *Innocence of Muslims*, a justified and appropriate response to insults directed at sacred religious figures? The question I am raising is one of degree: neutrality in the face of an insult directed at a religious leader might be a form of insipid injustice. The question I am raising is also one of situational ethics. Rioting is an antisocial and criminal act. Desmond Tutu's warning is right, but there are times and places, and there is an onus on believers of any faith to tread metaphorical minefields of appropriate and inappropriate response in any given context of injustice in our century no less than that of John the Seer.

John was not writing a code, strictly speaking, but he could be tantalizingly elusive. When he refers to a "beast with seven heads and ten horns" (Rev 17:7), he is alluding not only to the famous seven hills of Rome, but to seven Caesars (Rev 17:9–10). Of these, he tells us, "five have fallen, one is living, and the other has not yet come; and when he comes, he must remain only a little while" (Rev 17:10). This description should provide us with an accurate date for John's vision, yet he escapes any attempt to anchor his vision in time. Combinations of Caesars have been proposed, the most logical being Julius (emperor 49-44 BCE), Augustus (27 BCE –14 CE), Tiberius (14–37 CE), Gaius (37–41 CE), and Claudius (41–54 CE) as the five fallen, Nero (54–68 CE), who was known to have instigated a great persecution of Christians, the sixth, and Galba (June 68–January 69 CE) the one correctly

---

15. Cited by R. M. Brown, *Unexpected News*, 19.
16. The *Directoire exécutif* ruled France from 1795–1799.
17. Monaco, *Understanding Society*, 100–102.

foretold as reigning for "only a little while." While this shows remarkable prescience on John's part, Emperor Galba was followed in quick succession by Otho (January–April 69 CE) and Vitellius (April to December 69 CE), both of whom also reigned briefly, suggesting that John's gift of prescience was limited. There was also a considerable hiatus between the reigns of Julius and Augustus Caesar, presided over by the Second Triumvirate, breaking John's visionary succession.[18] John, it seems was not producing either a manifesto for political action or a template for historical analysis.

These details need not detract from the remarkable tenacity and timelessness of John's vision: the persecution of the Christian community by figures like Nero would resurface from time to time in the Roman Empire and in many empires since, and such an interpretation is faithful to John's own penchant for using the number "seven" as shorthand for "an allotted number." The violent overthrow of the one who John calls the "eighth but it belongs to the seven, and it goes to destruction" (v. 11) is consistent with the fate of many of the Caesars: Julius Caesar (assassinated), Caligula (assassinated), Claudius (probably murdered), Nero (suicide), Galba (assassinated), Otho (suicide), and Vitellius (lynched) all died violent and untimely deaths. The Jesus saying, recorded by Matthew, "all who take the sword will perish by the sword" (Matt 26:52), was unending, and John knew it (Rev 13:10). Adolf Hitler, Nicolae Ceausescu, Saddam Hussein, Muammar Gaddafi: all these and more have died in a manner that testifies to the timelessness of the vision of John and the saying of Jesus.

Even without getting bogged down in fatuous interpretations of the EEC as fulfillment of biblical prophecy, it is possible to become too deeply immersed in the serial symbols of power that John uses to depict the corrupting potential of state power structures. It is possible to be so focused on identifying, for example, the "ten horns who will receive power," that we fail to see the politico-historical wood for the trees. There will be, John tells his audience, corruption of power; it was centuries later that Shakespeare's megalomaniacal Richard III would find himself "So far in blood that sin will pluck on sin,"[19] but the potential for unimpeded power to fester and

---

18. Mounce, *Revelation*, 316, while reaching the same conclusion that the list is symbolic, argues that "the five who have fallen would be Augustus, Tiberius, Caligula, Claudius and Nero. The one who is would be Vespasian, and Titus would be the one to come." To confuse matters more, "Caligula" is Gaius Julius Caesar Augustus Germanicus, therefore Gaius; "Vespasian" is Titus Flavius Caesar Vespasianus Augustus. Mounce omits the rival trio of Galba, Otho, and Vitellius.

19. *Richard III*, Act 4, Scene 2.

It Is Done! (Revelation 15:1—20:15)

corrupt is timeless. It would be some centuries even after Shakespeare that Lord Acton would find the pithy phrase "all power corrupts and absolute power corrupts absolutely," but the phenomenon Lord Acton articulated is universal, and John was witnessing the serial corruption of the Roman state. Authority's transference into corruption is timeless: the corruption of authority that was happening in North Korea as I first wrote this section may or may not have been a transmission of tyranny from one generation to the next (though the signs are that the despotism of North Korea shows no sign of abating under the new regime of Kim Jong-un), but tyranny will always be, somewhere, sometime, a part of human experience. John is borrowing the symbolism of Daniel, who in Dan 7:7–8, 20, 24 foretold endless transmissions of corruption (Robespierre gives way to the Directors, Mubarak to the army). It would be impossible to find a period in history in which, somewhere on the globe, tyranny has not held sway for its "hour" (many fear that the Taliban are merely biding their time in Afghanistan, awaiting the withdrawal of UN troops. One might ask in any case whether the Hamid Karzai regime is devoid of tyrannies).

John will not allow his audience the terrible fear that tyranny has the last word. Contrary, often, to all appearances, the Lamb will indeed conquer.[20] This is a recurrent scriptural message,[21] and John knew that his audience would hear the allusion to the Hebrew prophets' predictions of divine victory. He also knew that the Christian community understood the ultimate divine victory not in terms of political overthrow, but the remarkable image of a crucified criminal, the Lamb of John's writings, overthrowing all that is evil. The whore of John's vision is merged with Jezebel of 1 Kgs 21:23–24 and 2 Kgs 9:10, 36–37, a figure of loathing to the Hebrew consciousness, until all evil is destroyed.

In chapter 18 John accumulates image after image of that pending destruction. The sheer accumulation of images serves a psychological effect, encouraging by utter weight of imagery an atmosphere of optimism in the hearts of those struggling to persevere in faith. In Rev 18:1–4 John uses a form of prophetic taunt[22] familiar to the audience from other Scripture passages.[23] Those who take to themselves the mantle (or cap) of Babylon *will* one day fall. Subsequent history supports John, as he knew past history

---

20. Rev 17:14, cf. 16:14–16, 19:19, 20:8–9.
21. Ezek 38:7–9, 39:2, Ps 2.
22. Aune, *Revelation 17–22*, 976.
23. Such as 1 Sam 17:4–5, Isa 23:15–6, 37:22–29, Jer 22:14–15, or Amos 5:1–3.

had. The original Babylonian Empire overreached itself—in his theology it ceased to be useful in the purposes of God—and collapsed in the ashes of its own entropy. This is a recurrent historical motif skillfully captured by some of the greater hymnists: at the height of the British Empire, on which the sun never set, hymn-writer and liberal-evangelical John Ellerton (1826–1893) reminded his people that the politics of empire were subservient to the processes of God:

> So be it, Lord; Thy throne shall never,
> like earth's proud empires, pass away:
> thy kingdom stands, and grows forever,
> 'till all Thy creatures own Thy sway.

Ellerton's was a brave reminder that human empires are transient. His words, like those of John, were all the more remarkable for being written at a time when there was no chink in the armor of the respective empires, and imperial jingoism was the rule of conversation. An earlier hymn-writer, Isaac Watts (1674–1748), writing before the great colonial (and missionary) expansion, avoided all reference to temporal kingdoms as he celebrated an eternal reign:

> Jesus shall reign where'er the sun
> doth his successive journeys run;
> his kingdom stretch from shore to shore,
> 'till moons shall wax and wane no more.

These two hymnic visions capture something of John's theology of hope, especially as it is expressed in the pileup of images in chapter 18.

The problem of the implementation of John's visions of victory comes about when the reign of God is confused with the reins of human politics, and theocratic yearnings begin to shout with authoritarian accents, rather than to whisper the words "it is finished" from a place of powerlessness. Those words were spoken not from a Kremlin or a White House, but from the cross of a powerless criminal. John repeats them as they are spoken from the celestial temple at Rev 16:17, but their origins in the cross of powerlessness are inescapable. The warning of Jürgen Moltmann is abiding:

> Reading the Bible with the eyes of the poor is a different thing from reading it with the eyes of a man with a full belly. If it is read in the light of the experience and hopes of the oppressed, the

It Is Done! (Revelation 15:1—20:15)

Bible's revolutionary themes—promise, exodus, resurrection and spirit—come alive.[24]

Until we remember this, we will forget that far too often, as the book of Revelation points its finger of judgment at the Beast, we are nestling in his pocket, rather than praying with the frightened saints. We may at the very least be the church at Sardis, whether we are Pentecostal or traditional in faith. As police do their job, obeying orders as they must, marching on the Occupy protestors of Wall Street and the world, we might ask whether the protestors or those gathering to ring the bell at the close of trading are closer to the ones who are to be saved out of Babylon's pockets (Rev 18:4).

Babylon who "glorified herself and lived luxuriously" will receive "a like measure of torment and grief." Babylon who in her heart used the language of dominance, saying "I rule as a queen; I am no widow, and I will never see grief" (Rev 18:7), was a political dominatrix, over whom not only the kings of the earth (Rev 18:9), but the merchants of the earth (Rev 18:11) weep bitterly. A US trade union song written by Florence Reece during the mining struggle of the 1930s put the question "which side are you on, boys, which side are you on?" Desmond Tutu's reference to mice and elephants' tails might have been informed by Florence Reece herself, except that this is the never ending question of struggles for justice: "there are no neutrals there," Reece observes, drily.[25]

While John suggests that human revolution breeds only more cycles of blood and hatred, this is also the eternal question put by the book of Revelation: which side are you on in a final revolution that is beyond human?

As we pass Rev 18:6, we need to pause at the language of retributive justice used there. Is this, like the call to take sides, a template for our behavior? The angel from heaven (Rev 18:1) cries out that Babylon is to have rendered to her "as she herself has rendered," and to be repaid "double for her deeds." It is, as so often is the case, an allusion by John to a Hebrew scriptural text, Jer 50:29. Yet to avoid the cycles of revolutionary blood alluded to throughout this study—and exemplified by the brutal deaths of the Caesars of John's cryptic timeline—we must hold the vision of punitive justice in parallel with the scriptural warning "vengeance is mine" (Deut

---

24. Moltmann, *Church*, 17.

25. The song, popularized by Pete Seeger, is alluded to by Bob Dylan in the apocalyptic vision of "Desolation Row," is sung by Natalie Merchant on her 2003 album *the House Carpenter's Daughter* and by Ani DiFranco as title track on her 2012 album *Which Side Are You On?* J. H. Claire was Sheriff of Harlan County in the 1930s.

32:35). This is picked up by both Paul (Rom 12:19) and the author of Hebrews (Heb 10:30).

Even Socrates, as depicted by Plato (in *Crito*, 49 BC) argued against retributive justice, though he never read Exod 21:23–25. In context, Exod 21:23–25 represented a restriction on retributive cycles of violence, but it may well be asked whether even that restriction has succeeded in breaking endless repetitions of payback, either in traditional or contemporary cultures. It has been argued that the Christian doctrine of grace, with implications for cessation of payback, was the major attraction to Christianity for the first Māori to hear the gospel proclaimed. Ngāpuhi, one of the dominant power forces in pre-European tribal warfare, were tired of protecting themselves from cycles of tribal payback and retributive justice, and they saw in the cycle-breaking words of Jesus, "turn the cheek" (Matt 5:38–42), an opportunity for peace. Auckland academic Christopher Honoré is cautious, however:

> According to [Harrison] Wright, another possible influence affecting Māori acceptance of the gospel was Ngāpuhi war-weariness consequent on the up to fifteen years of almost constant long expeditions to the south to contend with Ngāti Whātua, Ngāti Paoa, Arawa, the peoples of Ngāiterangi and Ngāti Porou. This might describe Ngāpuhi, but it does not sufficiently explain the rapid conversions in the Waikato [200–300 kilometers south of the primary missions].[26]

Payback is a significant principal of jurisprudence in many Australian-Pacific cultures. No matter what the official national law is, I am painfully aware that it plays a significant role in, for example, Australian Indigenous cultural practice, and that this has not been significantly altered by the imposition of Balanda law or faith. In my work as chaplain in a school community with a significant Indigenous population (some two hundred students, mainly boarding), I am aware of the degree to which payback plays a part in the "bush law," not only in the remote communities from which many students are drawn, but in the students' own daily processes of community living.

For the Christian community there is, even in the vivid scenes of John's vision, no room for retributive justice. Vengeance is mine, says God, and the New Testament option is to break cycles of retribution.[27] Punitive action is to be the right of God alone, and in the light of universalist texts such

26. Honoré, "Foundations," 41.
27. Rom 12:17, 1 Cor 6:7b, 1 Pet 3:9.

It Is Done! (Revelation 15:1—20:15)

as Rom 11:32 and 2 Pet 3:9, it is particularly important for us not to draw boundaries across the forbearance of God. This of course, once more, does not imply that in the sight of evil we bury our heads in the sand: practitioners and advocates of restorative justice, the more Christlike alternative to retributive justice, do not seek to wave magic wands and thereby erase bad happenings from history. Blood begets blood, but complacent silence also begets blood. The Way of the Cross will always be a way that speaks out, but (perhaps except *in extremis*) it will always look to Christlike non-violence to perpetrate the values of God. The book of Revelation, again and again, places final judgment into the hands of a celestial judge. On this side of the events depicted by John, it is the task of the followers of Christ to speak words of reconciliation and restitution, not retribution.

As Babylon falls (and all who wear her cap do likewise), the merchants of the earth weep with the kings. Here there is a warning for the nations of today's world, nations that have accrued to themselves wealth and power at the expense of the nations and cultures they have exploited. Rome, in John's time, was the center of commerce. This, surely, is a warning that reverberates with far more authority than the bell that closes Wall Street's trade? Prophetic and discomforting New Zealand poet James K. Baxter, perhaps with prescience foreseeing the me-now generations that followed the hippie revolts of the 1960s, spoke in his best-known poem of a young man who would grow up "to vote on the side of the bosses": which side are you on? "Love is not valued much in Pig Island" (slang for the more economically advantaged North Island of New Zealand), says Baxter, ruefully, "though we admire its walking parody."[28] As the Occupy protestors have seen—even if they have not altogether articulated alternatives to the *status quo*—paradigms of love, compassion, and justice are not necessarily proclaimed as the bell rings each night on Wall Street.

"Alas, alas, the great city, where all who had ships at sea grew rich by her wealth! For in one hour she has been laid waste," lament the onlookers in John's vision (Rev 18:19) in an allusion to the fall of Tyre of Ezek 27:32, and to every empire's fall. John may have deliberately chosen language that reminded his audience of the Great Fire of Rome (64 CE), almost certainly fresh in their memories even without the dubious advantages of contemporary media. But he is now simply recapitulating, image upon image, to demonstrate God's ability to decimate corrupt and exploitative human institutions. As the destruction ceases silence descends, but like "the day the

---

28. "Pig Island Letters," in Baxter, *Collected Poems*, 277.

music died" of Don McLean's poetic dreaming,[29] this is not a fertile and creative silence but the utter silence of a valley of dry bones or of Jeremiah's God-forsaken land (Jer 25:10). This is the place of no further joy, celebration, or hope: abandon hope all ye who enter here.

Juxtaposed to the sterile silence of hopelessness is the song of heaven that breaks out from Rev 19:1 onwards. This is the first Christian usage of a word familiar in subsequent Christian circles, "hallelujah" ("Praise YHWH"). The word is used more than a hundred times in the Hebrew Scriptures, and it takes John's audience in to the deepest, most visceral utterances of praise. For those who have experienced the utter timeless ecstasy of genuine Pentecostal worship there will be a familiar ring to this, but it is experienced, too, in the heights of formal liturgical praise. Once, as my wife Anne and I prayed at Evensong in St. Paul's Cathedral, London, we heard the cantor Lucy Winkett's voice rise into the heights of the famous and iconic dome; it was as if, as the philosopher Bergson would agree, time stood still. It was also as if, as Christmas and Easter liturgies say (echoing Ps 85), heaven kissed earth. Here, in John's vision, eternity is viewed and expressed as song, because words can never really say enough. We are beginning to pick up the rhythms of the crescendo of John's vision of eternity:

> For the Lord our God
> the Almighty reigns.
> Let us rejoice and exult
> and give him the glory (Rev 19:6–7).

Now, just as John has drawn liberally on Hebrew apocalyptic texts to flesh out his macabre vision of the destruction of evil, he draws on texts and references to flesh out his vision of eternal blessedness. From Rev 19:1–9 we are invited to be the tenth leper, to be a people of thanksgiving with praise that echoes through the eternities—and of which the worship that we generate this side of the *eschaton* should be pre-enactment. There is no room for misdirected worship (Rev 19:10); this is worship of the one who has transformed our lives from darkness to light and who will be that light eternally (Rev 21:23).

In Rev 19:11 John finally depicts the return of Jesus, his final and victorious coming in conquest. Once again it is worth recalling that this celestial scene has as its focus a criminal crucified by the Roman authorities within living memory of some members of John's audience, perhaps of John

---

29. The words form the introduction to the chorus line of Don McLean's, "American Pie," title track of his 1971 album.

It Is Done! (Revelation 15:1—20:15)

himself. Now Jesus comes (John uses the present tense) as judge, dividing good from evil. There is, *contra* much Christian complacency, but *pace* Roman Catholic doctrine, no room either for self-satisfaction or for terror in this vision: "blessed assurance" perhaps, but not blessed complacency. Christians whose proclamation of Christ has more closely epitomized the politics of hate than Christlike love (I think of those from the infamous Westboro Baptist church who stand on a US street proclaiming "God hates faggots," or who picket the funerals of those they condemn[30]) may have a little explaining to do. So might we all: where Christ was hungry, did we feed him? Naked, clothe him? When Patrick White was trying to find Christ did we welcome him, or tell him he was too gay, too decadent, too inclined to count beans in a jar?

We will all in this "moment in time outside of time" have some sorry-saying to undertake: we in the global north of Christianity have nestled far too deeply in the pockets of Jezebel. But no person, in global north or global south, is perfected: the blood that turned rivers red in the Rwanda genocide was the blood of Christians slaughtered by Christians, Tutsi and neutral Hutu Christians slaughtered (many as they cowered in churches) by Hutu Christians in a nation that was, statistically, one of the most Christian nations on earth. The blood that spilled in the Reformation of Europe was Christian blood spilled by Christians, even if the perpetrators (on all sides) had to discredit the faith of their victims before they died. The blood that is figuratively spilled as I overeat each night while others starve is often the blood of my fellow believers, those the Bible teaches me to call "brothers and sisters in Christ." And in any case, blood is blood is blood: when notional Christians slaughtered Muslims in Sarajevo in the Bosnian War or at Jerusalem in the Crusades, blood was blood was blood. Despite the ludicrous pastime of one or two scientists who still insist on seeking a "religion gene" or "God gene,"[31] the cross of Christ is not imprinted in the corpuscles of believers, and the DNA of a Moslem is the DNA of a Hindu is the DNA of an atheist. Or, we might say in the Judeo-Christian tradition, the *imago dei* (image of God) of a Moslem is the *imago dei* of a Hindu is the *imago dei* of an atheist.

The judgment images of Revelation, then, are not a cozy invitation to saunter into God's eternity. Neither though are they a thing of terror: the

---

30. See, e.g., "Kan. Church Plans to Picket Child Funerals." November 18, 2010. Online: http://www.koco.com/Kan-Church-Plans-To-Picket-Child-Funerals/-/9844716/10745494/-/51yo7s/-/index.html. See also the church's own website, http://www.godhatesfags.com/.

31. Wade, "Evolution."

Babylon's Cap

Christ who conquers evil and dismisses it to sulfur (Rev 19:20) dismisses the evil within us, leads us through the ambiguities of restorative justice, and into the eternities of God. This is what Paul means when he writes "What is sown is perishable, what is raised is imperishable" (1 Cor 15:42). It is also what he means when he writes, in the same apocalyptic passage (1 Cor 15:54–58),

> When this perishable body puts on imperishability, and this mortal body puts on immortality, then the saying that is written will be fulfilled:
> "Death has been swallowed up in victory."
> "Where, O death, is your victory?
> Where, O death, is your sting?"
> The sting of death is sin, and the power of sin is the law. But thanks be to God, who gives us the victory through our Lord Jesus Christ. Therefore, my beloved, be steadfast, immovable, always excelling in the work of the Lord, because you know that in the Lord your labor is not in vain.

John may not have read Paul, though there is little doubt he knew of his writings, but he is (like Paul) saturated in Old Testament and inter-testamental texts. His image of the victorious Christ owes much to the deutero-canonical book of Wisdom:

> your all-powerful word leaped from heaven, from the royal throne,
> into the midst of the land that was doomed,
> a stern warrior
> carrying the sharp sword of your authentic command,
> and stood and filled all things with death,
> and touched heaven while standing on the earth (Wis 18:15–16).

Our existence is "the land that was doomed," and it is into that state of hopelessness that Christ breathes eternity, first "rumored" at the first Easter, but completed and "installed" in John's vision of the end of time.

The scenes that follow in Rev 20 are images of the destruction of evil—not least the evil that most of us should acknowledge remains a potential within our own lives. Rev 20:10 is, as it happens, the sentence in the entire New Testament that most emphatically refers to any form of "eternal torment." But John's vision does not depict the eternal torment of individuals, of the Stephen Dedalus (or James Joyce) figure who slunk away from hellfire and damnation sermons. It is the destruction of evil systems, not individuals, and

It Is Done! (Revelation 15:1—20:15)

it is "highly symbolic language that is not intended to be taken literarily."[32] This is the end of evil, personified in comprehensible images. It is destroyed like carrion, as the birds from Ezek 39:17–20 destroy all that is unholy, unrighteous, and destructive in and around us. All that is at enmity with God is put to death in what John depicts as a final battle, Armageddon.

Millennialist Christians, particularly in the US, and most chillingly represented in the figure of Ronald Reagan, have seen Revelation's Armageddon in a different way. They have externalized all that is terrifyingly "other" to them—in Reagan's case it was the Soviet Union, but these days it is more likely to be Islam—and seen it depicted as being defeated in a final battle with the forces of God. This is dangerous confusion that has often meant that right-wing elements in or influenced by the US have shown no interest in matters of social justice for humans or environmental justice for the earth and its species. God will win, God's will shall be done, so let it be. Such an interpretation drives a wedge between the cross and the return of Jesus: Moltmann saw the danger with characteristic lucidity:

> The "nuclear Armageddon" about which Ronald Reagan talked so darkly means annihilation of the world without the kingdom of God. The ecological end of the world which many people are afraid of, and not without cause, means the destruction of nature without a new creation.[33]

This view of the *eschaton*, favored by the religious right and "moral majority" of Jerry Falwell and others in the US and beyond, generates a dangerous studied nonchalance towards creation and the peoples of the earth. It does so because it reads the destruction of the earth and the removal of the "unsaved" to eternal torment as a preordained inevitability, the necessary corollary of the "raptured" removal and eternal salvation of the chosen. If American politics hasten this end by opposition to Arab interests throughout the Middle East (and encouragement of the State of Israel and any moves it might take not only to crush Islam but to erect a final Third Temple in Jerusalem), then so be it: it is as it should be, says this view. At this point

---

32. Marshall, *Beyond Retribution*, 182, n. 112. Marshall notes that "images of 'unquenchable fire' (e.g., Matt 3:12; Mark 9:43, 48) and 'undying worms' (Mark 9:48; cf. Isa 66:24) are also not meant to imply unending torture. Instead, they underline the fact that nothing can prevent the agents of destruction from completing their work, which is total obliteration (cf. Heb 10:27; 12:29). In every case the evocative and metaphorical nature of apocalyptic must be allowed for." Ibid. Marshall at this point is permitting space for an annihilative doctrine of divine punishment.

33. Moltmann, as cited in Peter Althouse, *Spirit*, 117.

we might ask again our question of the media we use for information and analysis: does their interest lie in profiteering and the exploitation of earth's resources, or in justice and compassion for the broken and wretched of the earth? "Which side are you on?" If international policies on the use of fossil fuels and the deforestation of the earth hasten a cataclysmic collapse of the earth's ecosystems then so be it: it is the foreordained precursor to Christ's final, eternal victory. This, however, is a dangerous reading of apocalyptic, removing it from the coordinates of Christ's commands to compassionate justice for the wretched of the earth: when I was naked, you clothed me.

I referred earlier in this study to the sadly misguided predictions of Harold Camping, but he is only one of an incessant chain of millennialist soothsayers who change faith into entertainment. Moltmann once more:

> the "great rapture" is at the center of eschatological interest: will it save believers before "the great tribulation," in the midst of it, or only afterwards? There are "pre-tribulationists," "mid-tribulationists" and "post-tribulationists"—for the initiated: "pretrib premils, "midtrib premils" and "posttrib premils." They are politicized through the moral majority of Jerry Falwell and others, who since the time of Ronald Reagan have linked this apocalyptic fundamentalism with the political right in the USA, and with the preparation for a nuclear Armageddon.[34]

This late twentieth-, early twenty-first-century theological variation on counting angels on a needle is an obscene distraction from and distortion of the main game of John's apocalyptic. The "pretrib premils," "midtrib premils" and "posttrib premils" are likely, in my terms, to find themselves with some "sorry-saying" to undertake in the withering light of judgment. While John's focus is on those who bear witness to the Christ who stands against corrupt human power structures, the Reagan-Falwell school of interpretation stands in a position of power and condemns those who are suffering to hell.

John strings together a catena of images borrowed from biblical (Hebrew scriptural) and classical literary sources to provide images of judgment and punishment, and of the separation of the redeemed from the damned. Keys, pits, chains, dragons, serpents, locks and seals, and the notion of "a thousand years" are simply images of the victory of God over all that is evil. The "trib" delineations that Moltmann parodies miss the point that "a thousand years" is neither more nor less than "the appointed time"

34. Moltmann, *Coming*, 159.

It Is Done! (Revelation 15:1—20:15)

(2 Pet 3:8), and that, as Moses learned, "God will do and be what God will do and be" (Exod 3:14-15). This is John's depiction of a God who is in control, a depiction all the more remarkable given that John was writing and seeing visions at a time when much was turning ugly for the Jesus movement. In Rev 20:4 John sees "the souls of those who had been beheaded for their testimony to Jesus" and the "resurrected martyrs" appearing as judges. Since the time of John the list has extended immeasurably, but it remains a motif of hope if we imagine that, under the guidance of the Lamb, figures such as Graham Staines, Dietrich Bonhoeffer, Thomas Becket, Janani Luwum (the archbishop of Uganda assassinated by Idi Amin), Oscar Romero, Martin Luther King, and countless others were to look with the piercing gaze of Christ into the soul of the persecutors and executors of the just, righteous, and loving (Rev 20:4). Their gaze is a gaze of restorative, rather than retributive justice, for theirs is the gaze of the Jesus who says "Father, forgive." At the same time as the gaze of restorative judgment is turned on the conspicuous perpetrators of evil, the Idi Amins and Adolf Hitlers and extremists of every flavor, it will be turned on the surreptitious perpetrators of evil, those not exposed by a media with vested interests (for it should not be forgotten that US orders are likely to have signed the death warrant for Oscar Romero). At the same time that a gaze of restorative judgment and justice is turned upon all perpetrators of evil, those perpetrators continue to have the freedom to refuse the loving gaze of Christ. We might ask once more: can hatred conquer love?

John gathers visions of judgment, borrowed from all the sources he has tapped throughout his vision. Ultimately his vision is leading not to the punishment of human individuals, but to the destruction of evil itself. His vision is depicting the "death of death and hell's destruction," as Welsh hymn-writer William Williams put it: *this* is the final outcome of the judgment of Christ. It is up to the Judge, and to the response of those whose stand in his withering, judging stare, to decide for life or death eternally: in that moment, even the perpetrators of history's most evil actions may surrender to the unstoppable love of Christ. For if they do not, it is questionable whether love wins at all. This moment in John's vision represents the final moment in which creation—or the human part of it—opts for God's "no" or God's "yes."

6

God's Yes (Revelation 21:1—End)

IF YOU WERE TO read each of the gospel accounts from beginning to end it is probable that, following each account of the death of Jesus, you would experience something of a shift of narrative style. You may be aware of it only subconsciously, but it will become obvious as you think about it. It is as if (and probably was because) Matthew, Mark, Luke, and John each did all they could to establish what we might call the "comparative historicity" of the public events of Jesus' life. They did so even given their narration of extraordinary, miraculous events, healings and nature miracles, as well as the wise pronouncements and sayings of Jesus' ministry, which they saw to be historic. Luke spends a significant amount of verbal energy anchoring the events of Jesus' life in the known narratives of the Roman Empire:

> Since many have undertaken to set down an orderly account of the events that have been fulfilled among us, just as they were handed on to us by those who from the beginning were eyewitnesses and servants of the word, I too decided, after investigating everything carefully from the very first to write an orderly account for you, most excellent Theophilus, so that you may know the truth concerning the things about which you have been instructed.
> In the days of King Herod of Judea . . . (Luke 1:1–5).

Stylistically Luke is ensuring that his account is given what today we might call something like narrative credibility (see also Luke 3:1). We can not even be sure that "Theophilus" existed: some scholars suggest this was just a stylistic device used by Luke to give the impression of writing to a specific and significant public individual, an official of the Empire. This stylistic

God's Yes (Revelation 21:1—End)

sophistication and the reduced sense of apocalyptic urgency led some scholars to devalue Luke's gospel-account in particular as a diluted form of Jesus' message and a watered-down version of the apocalyptic urgency at the heart of Jesus' self-understanding.

Mark was writing in a different style, with almost tabloid energy (those who claim we should use the King James Version because of its magnificent prose and poetry often do not realize that much of the scriptural writing is vernacular, at best). Mark was writing some time before Luke, and he uses the device of solemn pronouncement to open his narrative; "The beginning of the good news" (Mark 1:1) was a phrase ringing with all the gravitas of the birth of an heir to the throne. Matthew begins with the solemn, formal-sounding "An account of the genealogy" into the history of God's dealings with the Hebrew people. John, a more eloquent author, begins very differently, with a majestic poem that interweaves narratives of the eternal Logos, the "Word made flesh" on the one hand and the witness John the Baptist on the other. Later, in his closing sentences, he will sound a tone similar to that he affords the Baptizer when authenticating his own narrative sources: "This is the disciple who is testifying to these things and has written them, and we know that his testimony is true" (John 21:24).

These are stylistic devices used by the authors as they struggled for the attention of an audience familiar with competing truth claims. Many religions vied for attention in the marketplaces, literal and metaphorical, of the Roman Empire. The Christian evangelists had to find a means to get their word, which they saw as *the* Word, out there. It was no easy task, but some sort of historical anchorage for the events they narrated would do no harm.

This leads to what some theologians refer to as the "scandal of specificity"; revelation as a process is limited to a specific place in a specific time, and all people in all other places and times are challenged to accept or reject the specifics. It is not a popular perspective in a post-modern world of relativities and competing truth claims. I will leave that for the Christian apologists and missiologists to sort out, but the context in which we wade through the claims of the New Testament writers today is not vastly different to that in which they were writing. Occasionally, though, we may need reminding that the claim Jesus made upon his followers was not "think on these things," but the imperative "follow me." It was the experiential dimension, the sense of redemption and of reconciliation with God that was gained after positive response to that invitational command, not mere intellectual assent, which assured the early Christians of the truth claims of the gospel.

Babylon's Cap

When the gospel writers write the narratives that follow the death of Jesus, they know they have entered into an experiential dimension, and their narrative style inescapably alters. One of the reasons they worked so hard at establishing the "historicity" (I sometimes, in preaching, use the word "thinginess") or objective truth of their story is because the crescendo to which their story is reaching is "far beyond the power of human telling." Bianco de Sienna wrote of "the yearning strong / with which the soul shall long," which "shall far out pass the power of human telling."[1] The problem faced by the gospel writers is that, when they came to tell the climax of their story, there were neither words nor images to suffice, and the experience of the eyewitnesses of the post-Easter events was "far beyond the power of human telling." You may be familiar with the poetry of the hallucinogenic 1960s, or even the opium-soaked poetry of previous centuries, not least Samuel Taylor Coleridge's majestic but not altogether comprehensible "Kubla Khan":

> And from this chasm, with ceaseless turmoil seething,
> As if this earth in fast thick pants were breathing,
> A mighty fountain momently was forced:
> Amid whose swift half-intermitted burst
> Huge fragments vaulted like rebounding hail,
> Or chaffy grain beneath the thresher's flail . . .

Whether Coleridge's story of waking from an opium-inspired dream is true or not, the imagery of his poem is an attempt to capture a scene beyond the power of human telling. Under the circumstances he did quite well, and literature devotees have been grateful to Byron for eventually persuading Coleridge to publish the magnificent but perhaps unfathomable lines.

As it happens, Mark made no attempt to narrate the post-resurrection events. His gospel account originally ended with the terrible dark words "they said nothing to anyone, for they were afraid" (Mark 16:8). Or these *would* be terrible and dark words if they were the end of the story—I was almost tempted to write "if they were true." Mark knew only too well that the women's fear was not the final word. He did not know that you and I would hear the resurrection story, but he knew that slowly person after person was being transformed by that same encounter that seized the women and overcame their fear, that person after person was likewise being transformed like those women who (however tremulously) repeated the words "he is risen." Luke, Matthew, John: they added narratives describing the

1. From the hymn "Come Down, O Love Divine."

God's Yes (Revelation 21:1—End)

scenes that followed. But they were strange scenes, "far beyond the power of human telling," even when eventually they became the culmination of works that came to be known by the title "Gospel."

Our John, the visionary, inherits these problems. He inherits them, as I have suggested from the start, at the moment he obeys the command "write" (Rev 1:11). Like the gospel writers, he is writing a confessional narrative, the story of a life seized by the one who the church now named the Spirit of God (Rev 1:10). As Lesslie Newbigin put it, "Christian faith is not a matter of logically demonstrable certainties but of the total commitment of fallible human beings putting their trust in a God who has called them."[2] These moments that the New Testament writers are recounting are the moments in which "heaven kisses earth" (Ps 95:10), or as the ancient Easter liturgy puts it, "when heaven is wedded to earth and all creation reconciled to God." Even Paul, one of the more prosaic of New Testament writers, breaks into the language of doxology and adoration at crowning moments: "What no eye has seen, nor ear heard, nor the human heart conceived, what God has prepared for those who love him . . ." (1 Cor 2:9). These thoughts will not convince a skeptic, and are not designed to, for the language of faith is the language of response to a command: "follow."

Language has always struggled to depict blessedness and goodness. Milton wondrously tells the story of the fall in *Paradise Lost*, but struggles to maintain interest in *Paradise Regained*. Most readers find Dante's *Inferno* far more interesting than his *Paradiso*, and Milton's Satan is far more interesting a personality than Milton's God. Blessedness of a state or of an individual is all but impossible to convey attractively. A contemporary writer such as John Marsden makes "saintly" figures (Robyn, in his *Tomorrow* series) interesting through a depiction of their fallibility. Harry Potter is a flawed hero, and the near-perfect Hermione Grainger is given plenty of rough and fallible edges to ensure she is not *utterly* nauseating!

C. S. Lewis wisely stops his *Narnia* narratives as the children and all the "blessed" enter "further up and further in." As Aslan tells Lucy, "the term is over: the holidays have begun. The dream has ended: this is the morning."

> And as He spoke He no longer looked to them like a lion; but the things that began to happen after that were so great and beautiful that I cannot write them. And for us this is the end of all the stories, and we can most truly say they all lived happily ever after. But

---

2. Newbigin, *Proper Confidence*, 98.

> for them it was only the beginning of the real story. All their life in this world and all their adventures in Narnia had only been the cover and the title page: now at last they were beginning Chapter One of the Great Story which no one on earth has read: which goes on for ever: in which every chapter is better than before.[3]

Even so cautious a writer as Lewis falls into a sort of narrative ecstasy at this point, relying a little on his neo-Platonic formations to hint at the bliss of eternity, but ultimately closing as all of us must before entering the untellable story. J. K. Rowling leaves the now-adult Harry and his wife Ginny farewelling their children on a railway platform—magical, but not eschatological. It is no accident that Rowling ends her series with the eschatological affirmation "all is well,"[4] rich in all its echoes of Julian of Norwich's (and through her T. S. Eliot's) "all manner of things shall be well."[5] In the world of film the transition is, to a degree, more simple: even in a post-modern era of cynicism or at best rationality, the Tom Hooper-directed 2012 *Les Miserables* captures in its closing scenes images of resurrection if not John of Patmos's new heavens and new earth. But they can be no more than the projection of what is known—Revolution-era France—on and into what is unknown: the possibilities of life after death.

Resurrection, eternity: these are not the only realm in which words fail: attempts to write seriously of the pinnacle experiences of human sexuality also fail abysmally; they can appear banal, obscene, silly, or all three, but certainly largely unattractive. Even the self-conscious sensualist D. H. Lawrence did not altogether succeed in narrating the erotic successfully, and the mutual adoration of pudenda reaches almost cloying sentimentality in *Lady Chatterley's Lover*, no matter how beautifully it is written. Yet it is no wonder that the philosophical theologian Paul Tillich chose the language of *eros* to speak of the deepest mysteries of God. Lest this be seen to be too weird in our somewhat prudish faith communities of the twenty-first century, it should be added that Tillich "insists that identifying the erotic with the sexual empties the concept of eros of its distinctive content."[6] Our John, however, did not ostensibly, or certainly did not primarily, take the option of writing with and through the lens of *eros*.

---

3. Lewis, *Last Battle*, 183–84.
4. Rowling, *Deathly Hallows*, 607.
5. Eliot, *Collected Poems*, 206. The lines are from Mother Julian's *Sixteen Revelations of Divine Love* in the 1390s.
6. Irwin, *Eros*, 6.

God's Yes (Revelation 21:1—End)

John is faced with a problem even greater than that faced by the gospel writers. They at least had an historical narrative and an historical timeline to follow. From the moment of his obedience to the command to write, John has been operating in a realm of super-reality, beyond-reality. Lewis's Neo-Platonism leads him to speak of a reality greater than our own; it is that concept that drives Paul's "eye has not seen nor ear heard" construction and others like it. It may not be self-consciously Neo-Platonic, but the gospel writers are adopting a similar structure: something greater than mere reality is here, in the resurrection (and ascension) scenes, they are telling us. The trouble with apocalyptic is that this is true of the entire writing.

As he moves into his "after the end" narration, John's difficulties become even greater. How do we describe that which is indescribable, that which "no human heart has conceived"? We can not—but John has been told to write. Like a Salvador Dali, or like a Gustav Klimt, or like almost all Aboriginal art,[7] and indeed like eastern iconography in its own very different, almost reversed and sub-dimensional way, John moves to the broad brush strokes of the unimaginable. As he has throughout his visionary work, he turns to others' words to enlarge any that he can offer— "borrowing" their authority for himself. "I saw a new heaven and a new earth": the words are from Isa 65:17. Isaiah however depicted these as a future action: "I am *about* to create new heavens and a new earth." John in his vision has seen these as completed and, for want of a better word, inhabited new heavens and new earth.

This method of allusion, borrowing from texts, is a method of expansion. When T. S. Eliot wanted to depict the opposite of John's vision, a depiction of hell in "The Wasteland," he enlarges his own dark script by quotation after quotation, allusion after allusion to previous authoritative writers and thinkers (Dante, Baudelaire, Swift, Conrad . . . the list is enormous). John does the same, and as his depiction of the "new heavens and new earth" continues, his audience would have heard behind almost every word the words of Isaiah and other Hebrew Scriptures. Their words had inspired the Hebrew people for centuries, and the Christian community for a few decades; "I am about to create Jerusalem as a joy, and its people as a delight," says Isaiah's God and John's:

7. As I write, I have in front of me the reproduction of an artwork, *Akwelkerrmwerlkerr*, by Genevieve Kemar Loy, from the Utopia region of Central Australia. In its swirling abstraction it is as fine an expression of the ecstasies of eternity as I have ever seen. The piece may be seen reproduced in the *Australian Religious Diary 2012* (Melbourne: David Lovell Publishing) for the week of 1–7 January, 2012.

Babylon's Cap

> I will rejoice in Jerusalem,
> and delight in my people;
> no more shall the sound of weeping be heard in it,
> or the cry of distress.
> No more shall there be in it
> an infant that lives but a few days,
> or an old person who does not live out a lifetime (Isa 65:19–20).

Isaiah's vision was probably intended to be far more this-worldly than John's (see Isa 65:21), but that does not matter here. Isaiah was writing of a reconstituted earthly city. John (like Augustine after him) is writing of a celestial and eternal "city of God."

John is still casting gauntlets: this is an eternal city created in and by a single *fiat* of God. Greek and other ancient religions (including Mayan!) allowed for cycles of creation, destruction and re-creation: John will have none of it. God will create out of the chaos and nothingness of the End (as God created once before, out of chaos and nothingness, a Beginning), and that creation will be perfect and endless. There will be in this new creation no causes of terror ("the sea" of Rev 21:1c), no tears or death (see Isa 25:8) or crying or pain, no dark shadow on existence. There will, though, be relationship: "I will be their God and they will be my children." Nor is this the description of a static state, but of growth. Words fail, but lifeless, growthless images of beings on clouds playing harps (or, as I once saw on a Christian record cover, angels sitting in an alcohol-free bar drinking celestial Coca-Cola) are not in the mind of John as he writes his beatific vision. Beneath his own words are those of Isaiah, and Isaiah's words include verb after verb: acting, doing, growing:

> They shall *build* houses and *inhabit* them;
> they shall *plant* vineyards and *eat* their fruit.
> They shall not *build* and another *inhabit*;
> they shall not *plant* and another *eat*;
> for like the days of a tree shall the days of my people be,
> and my chosen shall long *enjoy* the work of their hands.
> They shall not *labor* in vain,
> or *bear* children for calamity;
> for they shall be offspring *blessed* by the LORD—
> and their descendants as well.
> Before they *call* I will *answer*,
> while they are yet *speaking* I will *hear*.
> The wolf and the lamb shall *feed* together,
> the lion shall *eat* straw like the ox;

God's Yes (Revelation 21:1—End)

> but the serpent—its food shall be dust!
> They shall not hurt or destroy
> on all my holy mountain,
> says the LORD (Isa 65:21–25).[8]

Isaiah's this-worldly vision is in John's hands imbued with eternity, but Isaiah's verbs continue to resonate through John's sentences. John is not alone in adopting active images of eternity, of course: Jesus' own images of eternity begin with banquet scenes, hardly the stuff of static immobility.

In Rev 21:3 John deliberately picks up the structure and language of God's promise to the people of God in Ezek 37:26–27. That, too, was a divine promise spoken by an active God to an active people. That passage too is about eternity and action in an eternal dimension: "I will make a covenant of peace with them; it shall be an everlasting covenant with them; and I will bless them and multiply them, and will set my sanctuary among them forevermore." The "it" of "it is finished" (Rev 21:6) is all that is temporary, including all waiting and suffering, doubting and fearing. The verb is different in Greek to that used by Jesus on the cross, but the reiteration may be deliberate. Jesus' cry on the cross, *tetelestai*, is the declaration that God's estrangement from humanity is healed, but in Revelation's reiteration of the idea, rendered *gegōnan* (cf. Rev 16:7), the scar tissue, too, is gone. Twenty years ago I had a tumor removed from my shoulder: the thirty-centimeter scar is sometimes irritating, but far preferable to the tumor that was excised! In John's vision the scar tissue, too, is gone. In more traditionally theological terms, the hiatus between the final battle and victory day is over.[9] Cullmann, together with his near-contemporary Werner Georg Kümmel,[10] instigated into theological and biblical discourse the notion of "caught between the already and the not yet": the *tetelestai* of the cross, the delivery of the knockout blow in the final battle, is the "already." The *gegōnan* of Revelation is the signing off of victory day, the "not yet."

After making clear that the coming city of God, the New Jerusalem, is not a dwelling place of evil (Rev 21:8), John takes the risk of depicting his final vision of the un-static state of the blessed. If not actually utilizing the language of *eros*, John at least makes an allusion to erotic attraction, as he like many others depicts the final redemption of humanity in terms of the attraction of bride for groom, groom for bride. The bride of Rev 21:9 is

8. Italics mine.
9. Cullmann, *Salvation*, 44.
10. Kümmel, *Theology*.

133

Babylon's Cap

the city rather than, as in John 3:29, or as in the parables or the teachings of Eph 5, the church. As the church, she is captured poignantly in Samuel Stone's evocative hymn "The Church's One Foundation": the bride differs, but the tender and erotic narrative of attraction is the same. This is completion, a far more complete completion than that foreshadowed in the human experience of sexual union. D. H. Lawrence transformed sexual union into the ultimate homecoming—goodness knows, countless literary escapades have!—but John must respond with the knowledge that sexual union is mere fleeting encounter compared to the eternity of union he saw in his "prophetic trance."[11]

When, in my angst-ridden and atheistic adolescence, I first discovered the tender erotic longing and quasi-fulfillment of *Lady Chatterley's Lover*, its sexual imagery was as complete an image of human fulfillment as I could imagine. On my mental bookshelf it sat alongside a lyric from the "prog rock" band Emerson, Lake, and Palmer (though this lyric is attributed primarily to Greg Lake and Peter Sinfield), in which the singer pleads achingly with a "Divine and universal whore", crying out for sexual and spiritual fulfillment, or "completion," as the song refers to it.[12] I do not criticize sexual longing, only emphasize that it is perhaps the most powerful metaphor available to us to convey human experiences of attraction. "Magnetism" might equally suffice, but it somehow lacks the poetry!

Even if I have said that John eschews the language of the erotic, it is this kind of erotic, though not sexual and much less genital, longing that undergirds John's eschatological vision. Lake and Sinfield's erotically charged song of adolescent longing evokes a "divine and universal whore." I know nothing of Lake or Sinfield's knowledge of Christian Scriptures, but they have instinctively intertwined the apocalyptist's image of evil, the great and universal whore-figure of Rev 17 and 19:2, into their language of sexual completion and fulfillment. John's use of the imagery of whoredom was as much as anything the whoredom of economic evil, but deification of sexuality can be equally exploitative and destructive, equally life-denying, becoming, as Luke Timothy Johnson calls it, "the idolatrous pansexuality and addictive hedonism of the present age."[13] The deification of anything or anyone other than the Lamb is whoredom in John's theological world

---

11. Aune, *Revelation 17–22*, 1135.

12. Lake and Sinfield, "Lend Your Love to Me Tonight," from the Emerson, Lake and Palmer album *Works*, Atlantic,1977.

13. Johnson, *Creed*, 99.

God's Yes (Revelation 21:1—End)

view. This includes the deification of masculist power that leaves many women and children entrapped in the sex trade, many women entrapped in marriages not of mutual enrichment and edification but of violence and exploitation, or Pakistani teenager Malala Yousafzai fighting for her life after an assassination attempt by Taliban opposing her advocacy of education for girls. It is also the deification of heterosexist power that leaves gay people condemned to otherness or to outsider status in the narratives of the churches.

In his description of the heavenly city, John adopts the religious *lingua franca* of his time. The Qumran documents of the same period, for example, have much in common with John's celestial scene. This should not deter us: to describe anything, we must draw on the pools of language resources available to us or communication becomes meaningless. We are not now receiving a factual tour, of the type referred to by New Zealanders as "a Tiki Tour": "next we come to the Parliament Buildings." We are entering a symbolic journey into that which is far beyond description. The presence of a high mountain (Rev 21:10) near the Holy City is a literary necessity that represents both a visual vantage point (cf. Matt 4:8, Deut 34: 1–4) and the depiction of a place where holiness dwells. From there language of illumination and translucency broadly suggests the light of the presence of God, made specific at Rev 21:23 and 22:5. Jewels and gates and lengths and directions are accumulative imagery, forming impressions of eternity and opulence (but no longer decadence), serving again and again a visual equation of "all you can imagine but so much more." The images of a land enclosed by streams of living waters, with their echoes yet again of the language of the Fourth Gospel (John 4) are, as Milton saw clearly, images of paradise regained, of Eden re-entered but now illuminated purely by the glory of God. Here in this celestial vision anything that taints the purity of divine light is absent (Rev 21:27), and the face of God, on which in a fallen state no human could look and live, is now apparent to every dweller.

John has run out of words. Revelation 21:10—22:5 is an accumulation of ecstasy, John's beatific vision. These are Lewis's things that are "so great and beautiful that I cannot write them," the beginning of the real story. These are utterly beyond the power of human telling, though John will do and does do his best to hint at the vision's glorious and inexpressible ending.

Pie in the sky? The celestial vision can be seen only by the eyes of faith. Intellectually, rationally, this is incomprehensible. Like the six impossible things believed by the White Queen before breakfast,[14] these are risible images, unable to be quantified; these are, despite John's seemingly factual language of measurements and descriptive details of building materials, descriptions of "What no eye has seen, nor ear heard, nor the human heart conceived, what God has prepared for those who love him . . ." (1 Cor 2:9). Are they pie in the sky?

My answer to that question, as a pastor, a preacher, a priest, a chaplain, will never convince anyone. But it is no coincidence that as I have attempted to address the closing scenes of John's vision, I have found myself turning to the language of the erotic. These are scenes of consummation, but the consummation is no longer a merely biomechanical moment.

I happen to believe that at his best, D. H. Lawrence was a fine writer, though here I have used him as a foil to the universality of John's vision. Lawrence had long since rejected a Christianity that he saw as bland and life-denying; "the human body is only just coming to real life. With the Greeks it gave a lovely flicker, then Plato and Aristotle killed it, and Jesus finished it off," says Clifford, Connie Chatterley's highly symbolic impotent husband.[15] Lawrence posited sexual togetherness and consummation as the apotheosis of existence, not least because the Christianity of his youth had become a bland moralistic cerebralism. But he was wrong, certainly from the perspective of the apocalyptist John. The degree to which Lawrence's apotheosis of experience is limited is best revealed in an encounter with a lesser writer such as Henry Miller or Xaviera Hollander, whose narratives of sexual experience become little more than soporific once we have passed adolescence. Lawrence's characters battle against "the machine," a utilitarian society in which humans exist, antlike, merely as a commodity to serve the collective good: "it is a battle against the money, and the machine, and the insentient ideal monkeyishness of the world" muses the Lawrentian "hero," Mellors.[16]

Welsh poet R. S. Thomas suggests that God, too, must battle with "the machine that thinks it has outpaced belief."[17] For Thomas, the machine continues to urge annihilation, "urging me to cast myself / down into the abysm of secondary causation."[18] Thomas's poetry is often a dark struggle

---

14. Carroll, *Adventures*, 157–58.
15. Lawrence, *Lady Chatterley's Lover*, 245.
16. Ibid., 292.
17. "Directions," in R. S. Thomas, *Later Poems*, 131.
18. "Temptation," in R. S. Thomas, *Residues*, 65.

God's Yes (Revelation 21:1—End)

between the "abysm" of human existence and the beckoning of a God who leaves behind only warm footprints, but who summons humankind by mysterious "entelechy," an energy drawing creation forward into a machine-free future. John, in his letters to the churches, knows that one form of the machine is a vicious and life-denying brute that is the Roman Empire, but it is also *all* life lived without God. To John, Lawrence's or Lake's search for sexual fulfillment, sexual completion as the apotheosis of human meaning, is just one more sign of servitude to forces that are life- and hope-denying, servitude to the machine. John would have sung his amen to the words of nineteenth-century poet and hymn-writer Caroline Marie Noel, "In your hearts enthrone him; there let him subdue / All that is not holy, all that is not true." To do less is to be back in the church of Ephesus or Laodicea.

Entelechy? The word was probably coined by Aristotle and has been given various nuances in philosophical thought since. My own borrowing of it is from Teilhard de Chardin, though whether he actually adopted the word or it has been applied by others to his thought has long since eluded me. In many ways Teilhard is a backwater in Christian theology,[19] and as the owner of a non-scientific mind I found all his works except *Le Milieu Divin* incomprehensible. *Le Milieu Divin* I found mainly incomprehensible yet paradoxically inspirational (perhaps not unlike the book of Revelation for many of us!). If there is a theme that emerges from *Le Milieu Divin*, it is that all creation has built into its existence a volition, an entelechy, an irresistible forward-drawing energy towards its final Omega Point, its final consummation. Teilhard is not a great citer of Scripture, but his Omega Point approximates the "all in all" of 1 Cor 15:28. That in turn approaches the words of John's vision, "It is done! I am the Alpha and the Omega, the beginning and the end" (Rev 21:6). Teilhard of course borrowed his "Omega point" from Revelation, or perhaps we should say from the Greek alphabet from which John's vision borrows it. God is the Alpha and the Omega: towards God all time and all that dwells within time is being led by God's energies. These internal energies, planted in creation at its Alpha point, are as strong as the energies that drive the thirsty to drink (Rev 22:17).

19. Though one Teilhard scholar, Ingrid Schafer, notes "On July 20, 2002, a search of the terms 'Teilhard and Internet' in the EBSCO Host data base yielded 61 full text articles, primarily published since 1997; in the Google search engine the same terms resulted in 6,220 hits. Even the presumably obscure term 'noosphere' appears 16,800 times, with explanations ranging from 'The Emerging Web of Consciousness' to 'UFO-Seek' and 'The Astrology Directory.' Clearly, Teilhard is being discussed among a vast spectrum of admirers and critics, including scholars, computer scientists, New Age enthusiasts, and would-be Net-profiteers." Schafer, "Noosphere," 825.

Babylon's Cap

Hebrew Rabbinic scholarship delighted—delights—in the play of words. The horizontal arms of the Hebrew letter *bet* (ב), with which the Hebrew Scriptures begin, was seen to embrace all that follows (Hebrew reads from right to left) within the arms of the Creator, even to the end of time. Perhaps instinctively John, or those who placed his vision at the end of the canon of Scripture, adopted a similar technique, so that he concludes his mystical vision with the Aramaic "Amen," variously translated "truly" or "yes." Literary taste is a subjective matter, but for me the pinnacle of English literature has been James Joyce's magisterial *Ulysses*. It took Joyce years to write it, and he worked hard to ensure that his final word was "yes":

> I was a Flower of the mountain yes when I put the rose in my hair like the Andalusian girls used or shall I wear a red yes and how he kissed me under the Moorish wall and I thought well as well him as another and then I asked him with my eyes to ask again yes and then he asked me would I yes to say yes my mountain flower and first I put my arms around him yes and drew him down to me so he could feel my breasts all perfume yes and his heart was going like mad and yes I said yes I will Yes.[20]

This of course is the language of sexual surrender and consummation yet again (for what it is worth, I think Joyce achieves his aim of celebrating sexuality far more effectively because he does it far less self-consciously than Lawrence) but this should not surprise us. Sexual union is a created gift of God; it is only when the creature rather than the Creator becomes the focus of our adoration that our lives are skewed (Rom 1:2–25). Then we become perpetually enmeshed in Greg Lake's adolescent longing, and our journey to John's Omega point is, if not eternally severed (which I do not believe), nevertheless bogged unnecessarily in muddy backwaters. There is more than one way to be Laodicean.

But John's vision is ultimately and eternally positive. Christian interpreters have dwelt, especially in times of oppression or persecution, on the fiery vats and destruction of enemies. Those images, though, are primarily about the destruction of evil, not of individuals, and they are far less about the eternal destruction of Mr. Smith or Mrs. Brown down the road who might not share our faith. The apocalyptic vision of John is about God's victory over all that is evil, so that there shall be no more sorrow or tears or suffering. Unless radical amnesia is a part of God's eternal plan, then an incomplete membership of the new heavens and new earth (Rev 21:1) is

---

20. Joyce, *Ulysses*, 735.

God's Yes (Revelation 21:1—End)

not altogether good news, and someone, somewhere will spend eternity lamenting the absence of Mr. Smith or Mrs. Brown (as road safety ads imply, everybody is "somebody's son, somebody's mother"). No more tears, says Revelation: "mourning and crying and pain will be no more."

This may well be pie in the sky, of course: no one has ever returned from death or from the end of time to let us know. Yet at the time of John, and before and since the time of John, followers of Jesus, the one John calls the Lamb, have been prepared to live and die for this version of truth. They were prepared to do so because, inspired by John and other visionaries who were servants of the gospel, they believed that present experience in all its suffering was not the final word. The final word was God's "yes" to creation: The grace of the Lord Jesus be with all the saints. Amen.

Bibliography

A Prayer Book for Australia. Sydney: Broughton Books, 1985.
A New Zealand Prayer Book/He Karakia Mihinare o Aotearoa. Auckland: The Church of the Province of New Zealand, 1989.
Australian Council of Trade Unions. 2010. "Executive Paywatch 2010: Special Report by the ACTU." No pages. Online: http://www.actu.org.au/Publications/Other/ExecutivePayWatchReport.aspx.
Althouse, Peter. *Spirit of the Last Days: Pentecostal Eschatology in Conversation with Jürgen Moltmann*. New York: T&T Clark Continuum, 2003.
Aune, David E. *Revelation 1–5*. Word Biblical Commentary 52a. Dallas: Word, 1997.
———. *Revelation 6–16*. WBC 52b. Nashville: Thomas Nelson, 1998.
———. *Revelation 17–22*. WBC 52c. Nashville: Thomas Nelson, 1998.
Barnes, Julian. *Nothing to Be Frightened Of.* New York: Vintage, 2009.
Barth, K. *Church Dogmatics*. Translated by G.T. Thompson et al. Edinburgh: T. & T. Clark, 1936–77.
Bauckham, Richard. *The Theology of the Book of Revelation*. New Testament Theology. Cambridge: Cambridge University Press, 1993.
Baxter, James K. *Collected Poems*. Auckland: Oxford University Press, 1981.
Beckford, William. "Vathek." In *Three Gothic Novels*. Edited by Peter Fairclough. 149–255. Harmondsworth: Penguin, 1968.
Behrendt, Larissa. "Genocide: The Distance between Law and Life." *Aboriginal History* 1, no. 25 (2001): 132–47.
Bell, Rob. *Love Wins: A Book About Heaven, Hell, and the Fate of Every Person Who Ever Lived*. New York: HarperOne, 2011.
Borch, Merete. "Rethinking the Origins of Terra Nullius." *Australian Historical Studies* 32 (2001): 222–39.
Boring, Eugene M. *Revelation*. Westminster: John Knox, 1989.
Broome, Richard. *Aboriginal Australians*, 4th ed. Crows Nest (NSW): Allen & Unwin, 2010.
Brown, C. S. "T. S. Eliot and 'Die Droste.'" *The Sewanee Review* 46, no. 4 (1938): 493.
Brown, R. M. *Unexpected News: Reading the Bible with Third World Eyes*. Philadelphia: Westminster, 1984.
Brueggemann, Walter. *The Prophetic Imagination*. Phildalphia: Fortress, 1978.
Bullock, Alan. *Hitler and Stalin: Parallel Lives*. London: HarperCollins, 1991.
Camus, Albert. *The Fall*. Translated by Justin O'Brien. New York: Vintage, 1991.
Caroll, Lewis. *Alice's Adventures in Wonderland/Through the Looking Glass*. Harmondsworth: Puffin, 1962.

Bibliography

Charlesworth, James M. *Apocalyptic Literature and Testaments: The Old Testament Pseudepigrapha*. Garden City, NY: Anchor, 1983.
Clare, Cassandra. *City of Bones*. The Mortal Instruments. London: Walker Books, 2007.
———. *City of Ashes*. The Mortal Instruments. London: Walker Books, 2008.
Coombes, Andrea, "Wednesday's Personal Finance Stories." *MarketWatch* (*The Wall Street Journal*). No pages. Online: http://articles.marketwatch.com/2010-09-01/finance/30697394_1_wage-growth-median-weekly-wage-ceos.
Cullmann, O. *Salvation in History*. Translated by Sydney S. Stowers. London: SCM, 1967.
Davidson, J. P. *Planet Word*. London: Michael Joseph, 2011.
Debien, Noel. "First Complete Bible Translation in an Indigenous Language." *The Religion Report* (2007). No pages. Online: http://www.abc.net.au/radionational/programs/religionreport/first-complete-bible-translation-in-an-indigenous/3246340#transcript.
Defoe, Daniel. *Robinson Crusoe*. English Library. Harmondsworth: Penguin, 1970.
Dickens, Charles. *Bleak House*. Boston: Houghton Mifflin, 1958.
Donovan, Peter. *Religious Language*. Issues in Religious Studies. London: Sheldon Press, 1976.
Dylan, Bob. *Lyrics 1962–2001*. New York: Simon and Schuster. 2004.
Farrar, Frederick. *Eternal Hope: Five Sermons Preached in Westminster Abbey, November and December 1877*. New York: E. P. Dutton & Co., 1878.
Fiorenza, Elisabeth Schüssler. *Revalation: Vision of a Just World*. Edinburgh: T. & T. Clark, 1991.
Gardner, Helen. *The Composition of Four Quartets*. London: Faber and Faber, 1978.
Godfrey, Michael J. H. "Lizards and Clay." In *Encounter*, edited by Florence Spurling. ABC Radio National, 1996.
———. "Defoe's Ego Contra Mundum or 'the Dark Side of Crusoe's Eucharist'?" In *The Dark Side*, edited by Christopher Hartney and Andrew McGarrity, 71–88. Sydney: RLA Press, 2004.
Greene, Graham, *The Power and the Glory*. Harmondsworth: Penguin, 1969.
Eliot, T. S. *Collected Poems 1909–1962*. London: Faber and Faber, 1963.
Harrington, Wilfrid J. *Revelation*. Sacra Pagina 16. Collegeville: Liturgical Press, 1993.
Harris, John. *One Blood*. 2nd ed. Sutherland (NSW): Albatross, 1994.
Hitchens, Christopher. *God Is Not Great: How Religion Poisons Everything*. New York: Hachette BookGroup, 2007.
Honoré, Christopher. "Foundations: From Mission to Te Hāhi Mihinare (1814–45)." In *Living Legacy: A History of the Anglican Diocese of Auckland*, edited by Allan K. Davidson, 23–49. Auckland: Anglican Diocese of Auckland, 2011.
Irwin, Alexander C. *Eros toward the World: Paul Tillich and the Theology of the Erotic*. Minneapolis: Fortress, 1992.
Johnson, Luke Timothy. *The Creed: What Christians Believe and Why It Matters*. London: Darton, Longman & Todd, 2003.
Joyce, James. *A Portrait of the Artist as a Young Man*. Reprint. London: Grafton Books, 1977.
———. *Ullyses*. London: Folio Society, 1998.
Käsemann, Ernst. *Commentary on Romans*. Translated by G. W. Bromiley. London: SCM, 1980.
Kierkegaard, Søren. *Either/Or*. Translated by David Swenson et al. Vol. 1. Princeton: Princeton University Press, 1979.

Bibliography

Kingsolver, Barbara. *The Poisonwood Bible*. London: Faber and Faber, 2000.
Klostermaier, Klaus. *Hindu and Christian in Vrindaban*. London: SCM, 1969.
Kreider, Alan. "The Way of Christ." In *Is Revolution Change?*, edited by Brian Griffiths, 46–69. London: InterVarsity Press, 1972.
Kümmel, H. G. *The Theology of the New Testament: According to Its Major Witnesses, Jesus, Paul, John*. Translated by John H. Steely. London: SCM, 1974.
Lawrence, D. H. *Lady Chatterley's Lover*. 2nd ed. Harmondsworth: Penguin, 1961.
Lewis, C. S. *The Last Battle*. The Chronicles of Narnia. London: HarperCollins, 1998.
———. *The Lion, the Witch and the Wardrobe*. The Chronicles of Narnia. London: Puffin, 1970.
Lynch, John. *Pacific Languages: An Introduction*. Honolulu: University of Hawai'i Press, 1998.
Marshall, Christopher D. *Beyond Retribution: A New Testament Vision for Justice, Crime and Punishment*. Studies in Peace and Scripture. Grand Rapids: Eerdmans, 2001.
Massyngberde Ford, J. *Revelation*. Anchor Bible 38. Garden City: Doubleday, 1975.
Meacham, Jon. "Pastor Rob Bell: What If Hell Doesn't Exist?" *Time* (14 April 2011). Online: http://www.time.com/time/magazine/article/0,9171,2065289,00.html.
Moltmann, Jürgen. *Theology of Hope: On the Grounds and the Implications of a Christian Eschatology*. Translated by James W. Leitch. London: SCM, 1967.
———. *The Crucified God*. Translated by R. A. Wilson & John Bowden. London: SCM, 1974.
———. *The Church in the Power of the Spirit*. Translated by Margaret Kohl. London: SCM, 1977.
———. *The Coming of God: Christian Eschatology*. London: SCM, 1996.
Monaco, Paul. *Understanding Society, Culture and Television*. Westport, CT: Praeger, 1998.
Morris, Leon. *The Book of Revelation: An Introduction and Commentary*. TNTC. Leicester: InterVarsity Press, 1987.
Mounce, Robert H. *The Book of Revelation*. 2nd ed. NICNT. Grand Rapids: Eerdmans, 1997.
Ness, Patrick. *Monsters of Men*. Chaos Walking. London: Walker Books, 2010.
Newbigin, Lesslie. *Proper Confidence: Faith, Doubt, and Certainty in Christian Discipleship*. Grand Rapids: Eerdmans, 1995.
Nicholls, David. *Deity and Domination: Images of God and the State in the 19th and 20th Centuries*. Hulsean Lectures. London: Routlege, 1989.
Nietzsche, Friedrich. "On the History of Moral Feelings." In *Human, All Too Human*. 1878. Online: http://nietzsche.holtof.com/Nietzsche_human_all_too_human/sect2_on_the_History_of_Moral_Feelings.htm
Otto, R. *The Idea of the Holy*. 2nd ed. Oxford: Oxford University Press, 1958.
Pelikan, Jaroslav. *The Emergence of the Catholic Tradition (100-600)*. Vol. 1 of *The Christian Tradition: A History of the Development of Doctrine*. Chicago: University of Chicago Press, 1975.
———. *Reformation of Church and Dogma (1300–1700)*. Vol. 4 of *The Christian Tradition: A History of the Development of Doctrine*. Chicago: University of Chicago Press, 1984.
Postman, Neil. *Amusing Ourselves to Death: Public Discourse in the Age of Show Business*. British ed. London: Methuen, 1987.
Quinn, Richard. *Samuel Marsden: Altar Ego*. Wellington: Dunmore, 2008.
Ramsey, Ian T. *Religious Language*. London: SCM, 1967.

Bibliography

Rowland, Christopher. "Revelation." *The New Interpreter's Bible*, Vol. 12 (Hebrews to Revelation), 501–743. Nashville: Abingdon, 1998.

Rowling, J. K. *Harry Potter and the Deathly Hallows*. London: Bloomsbury, 2007.

———. *Harry Potter and the Order of the Phoenix*. London: Bloomsbury, 2003.

Russell, D. S. *Apocalyptic, Ancient and Modern*. The Hayward Lectures. London: SCM, 1978.

Ryan, Lyndall. *Tasmanian Aborigines: A History Since 1803*. Crows Nest (NSW): Allen & Unwin, 2012.

Schade, Joseph I. *Catholic Doctrine*. Paterson, NJ: St Anthony Guild Press, 1943.

Schafer, Ingrid. "From Noosphere to Theosphere: Cyclotrons, Cyberspace, and Teilhard's Vision of Cosmic Love." *Zygon: Journal of Religion and Science* 37, no. 4 (2002): 825–52.

Stanner, W. E. H. *White Man Got No Dreaming: Essays 1938–1979*. Canberra: Australian National University Press, 1979.

Thomas, R. S. *Later Poems*. 2nd ed. London: Macmillan (PaperMac), 1984.

———. *Selected Poems 1946–1968*, 12th ed. Newcastle Upon Tyne: Bloodaxe Books, 1997.

———. *Residues*. Highgreen: Bloodaxe Books, 2002.

Trible, Phylis. *Texts of Terror: Literary-Feminist Readings of Biblical Narratives*. Minneapolis: Fortress, 1984.

Trudgen, R. *Why Warriors Lie Down and Die*. Darwin (NT): Aboriginal Resource and Development Services, 2000.

van den Bosch, Lourens. "A Burning Question: Asti and Sati Temples as the Focus of Political Interest." *Numen* 37, no. 2 (1990): 174–94.

Volf, Miroslav. *Exclusion and Embrace: A Theological Exploration of Identity, Otherness and Reconciliation*. Nashville: Abingdon, 1996.

Vrankovitch, Mark. "Brian Tamaki's Destiny Church Is Now a Cult." No pages. Online: http://www.cultwatch.com/briantamaki.html.

Wade, Nicholas. "The Evolution of the God Gene." The Week in Review. *New York Times* (14 November 2009). No pages. Online: http://www.nytimes.com/2009/11/15/weekinreview/12wade.html?_r=0.

Walker, Alan. *The Contrast Society of Jesus*. Blackburn (VIC): HarperCollins, 1997.

Watson, Jessica. *True Spirit: The Aussie Girl Who Took on the World*. Sydney: Hatchette, 2009.

Watterson, W. *It's a Magical World: A Calvin and Hobbes Collection by Bill Watterson*. Kansas: Andrew McMeel, 1996.

White, Patrick. *Flaws in the Glass: A Self Portrait*. London: J. Cape, 1981.

Wilson, Bruce W. *Reasons of the Heart*. St Leonards (NSW): Allen & Unwin/Albatross, 1998.

Woodward, Bob. *Bush at War*. Reprint. New York: Simon and Schuster, 2003.

www.ingramcontent.com/pod-product-compliance
Lightning Source LLC
Chambersburg PA
CBHW060822190426
43197CB00038B/2196